Mastering Behavior-Driven Development Using Cucumber

Practice and Implement Page Object Design Pattern, Test Suites in Cucumber, POM TestNG Integration, Cucumber Reports, and Work with Selenium Grid

Pinakin A Chaubal

www.bpbonline.com

FIRST EDITION 2021

ISBN: 978-93-91030-476

LIMITS OF LIABILITY AND DISCLAIMER OF WARRANTY

Distributors:

BPB PUBLICATIONS
20, Ansari Road, Darya Ganj
New Delhi-110002
Ph: 23254990/23254991

DECCAN AGENCIES
4-3-329, Bank Street,
Hyderabad-500195
Ph: 24756967/24756400

MICRO MEDIA
Shop No. 5, Mahendra Chambers,
150 DN Rd. Next to Capital Cinema,
V.T. (C.S.T.) Station, MUMBAI-400 001
Ph: 22078296/22078297

BPB BOOK CENTRE
376 Old Lajpat Rai Market,
Delhi-110006
Ph: 23861747

Published by Manish Jain for BPB Publications, 20 Ansari Road, Darya Ganj, New Delhi-110002 and Printed by him at Repro India Ltd, Mumbai

www.bpbonline.com

Dedicated to

My beloved Parents:

Shri Ashok Anant Chaubal

Sulabha Ashok Chaubal

&

My beloved son Arnav

About the Author

Pinakin Chaubal is a BE (Computer Science) Graduate with over 19years of work experience in the IT domain. He is a certified PMP, ISTQB, HP0-M47 (QTP 11.0 Functional testing expert) and INS-21(General Insurance). He is working as an Automation Architect at Intellect Design Arena Ltd (earlier known as Polaris Consulting). Prior to this, he has worked with companies such as Patni, Accenture, ACS International (USA), L&T Infotech (USA & India), Polaris Financial Technology and SQS. He carries 6 years of onsite experience in the US and 8 months in Hong Kong and China working closely with the clients and being a part of senior management and stakeholder meetings. The clients that he has worked for include YES Bank, HSBC, Travelers Insurance, Harleysville insurance, Albertsons retail chain, Bellsouth Telecommunications, GE-Fleet Services, and GE-Supply. He is the creator of the YouTube channel 'Automation Geek', which teaches PMP, ISTQB, Test Automation using Selenium and Cucumber and Performance testing using JMeter 3.0. He is the author of 'Page Object Model using Selenium WebDriver and Java', 'Selenium WebDriver Quick Start Guide' published by Packt Publishing, and 'Selenium Framework design with Keyword Driven Testing' published by BPB Publications. He is also the reviewer of the newly released book on Selenium Frameworks - 'Selenium Framework Design in Data Driven Testing' by Carl Cocchiaro.

About the Reviewers

- **Narottam Singh** is a Software Development Engineer in Test with over 10 years of experience in delivering quality products. Currently, his responsibilities include end-to-end testing (manual and automation) of mobile apps on Android and iOS platforms.

  So far, he has got the opportunity to work on few hottest technologies in the software industry i.e., Elastic search, Kafka, OpenShift and Test Automation (Web, Rest-API and Mobile Apps). He has worked with JAVA, Python, Node.js , Selenium, Cypress.io and Linux programming languages for Test Automation.

  During his journey with various organizations, Narottam learned that quality of the product is utmost important for client and end-user satisfaction.

  He always believes that if something is built with quality paradigms, it makes the customer's life easy.

  LinkedIn: **https://www.linkedin.com/in/narottamgla**

  GitHub: **https://github.com/narottamgla**

- **Garima Chauhan** is a Software Development Engineer in Test with over 6 years of experience in implementing quality products. Currently, she is working for Walmart as a Quality Engineer III. She is responsible for end-to-end testing (manual and automation) of mobile apps on Android and iOS platforms.

  So far, she has worked in almost 5 verticals of testing i.e., Manual, Automation, Load, Performance and A/B testing. To deliver stable and bug-free products, she has started learning automation testing. She has worked with JAVA, Python, Selenium, JavaScript, Linux programming languages and implemented tests.

  Garima started her career with a B2B company RechargeItNow with manual testing as an Associate Quality Engineer. Later, she worked for Citrus Payments Solutions and PayU as a Lead Software Engineer for almost 5 years. She worked as a Lead Software Engineer in Test and delivered fully tested products to facilitate users a bug free experience during payments flow.

  All the products are live and are used by merchants like Hotstar, GoAir, Dream 11, NDTV Gadgets, Big Basket, Lenskart, Zee, Videocon and many more. . .

She worked for Sequoia Consulting Group which is a US based company that works in the health insurance and HR management domain. At this organization, she learned how to test or validate high volumes of sensitive data which is entirely a combination of manual and automation testing effort. She spent 1 year at this organization and learned different ways of testing and mainly worked on micro-services, API's and website portals.

Garima loves to spend time on testing things and her hobbies include traveling, yoga, and cooking.

She always believe that if something is built with quality paradigms, it makes the customer's life easy.

Acknowledgement

There are a few people I want to thank for the continued and ongoing support they have given me during the writing of this book. First and foremost, I would like to thank my parents for continuously encouraging me for writing the book — I could have never completed this book without their support.

I would like to thank Manasi, who is very special to me and who, during the entire course of writing this book provided me loads of positivity and support.

My gratitude also goes to the team at BPB Publications for being supportive enough to provide me quite a long time to finish the first part of the book. Thanks for allowing me to publish the book in multiple parts, since image processing, being a vast and very active area of research, was impossible to deep-dive into different class of problems in a single book, that too by not making it voluminous.

Preface

This book covers the Cucumber BDD test automation tool. BDD stands for Behavior driven development. BDD is an extension of TDD that makes use of a simple, Domain Specific Language (DSL). The DSL is in plain English and converts natural language statements into executable tests. The DSL that we are going to study in this book is known by the name Gherkin. The term Gherkin however is specific to Cucumber, JBehave, Behave and Behat software tools.

This book will be divided into three sections:

Section 1 will explore what Cucumber is along with the building blocks such as Feature files, Step Definition classes and Runner classes. These will form the foundation for getting up-to-speed with Cucumber.

Section 2 will explore the Page Object design pattern and make the reader understand Page Objects and Page Factories.

Section 3 will explore the integration part of Cucumber with TestNG and Maven. We will be putting the Maven build in Jenkins and thus configure Jenkins for automatic triggering on completion of a Dev build.

After reading this book, the test engineer will be conversant with incorporating Cucumber as a BDD framework in his testing and thus streamlining the testing and bug detection process.

Section I

Chapter 1 makes you understand the concept of Test Driven Development(TDD) followed by Behavior Driven Development(BDD).TDD stands for Test Driven Development.

Chapter 2, describes the Feature files which are the documents that contain Gherkin scenarios and requirements – they can be very useful to teams working on BDD. Feature file is a key deliverable for BAs. Feature files are where BAs store the requirements in Gherkin format and create the bridge between requirements and automated tests.

Chapter 3 describes about the Gherkin statements which are present in the Feature files and are translated into code using what is called a Step Definition. It is the bridge between the utility Java classes which will be the Page Objects and the Feature files. The Step Definition files contain regular expressions in addition to Java code.

Chapter 4 will cover the test runner class which also acts as an interlink between feature files and step definition classes. It is in the test runner class, that you provide the path for both feature file and step definition class.

Section II

Chapter 5 onwards, we will jump into action by first understanding the Page Object Design Pattern and Page Object Model. We will the create Page Objects for all the individual Web Pages in the Application Under Test[AUT]. A page object contains logic for working with all HTML objects on the Page.

Chapter 6 will cover the PageFactory Class in Selenium which is an extension to the Page Object design pattern. It is used to initialize the elements of the Page Object or instantiate the Page Objects itself. It is used to initialize elements of a Page class without having to use 'FindElement' or 'FindElements'. We will create Page factories fr static web elements.

Section III

Chapter 7 will cover TestNG in Selenium which is a testing framework in Java, inspired by JUnit and NUnit. It overcomes the constraints of JUnit. From simple unit testing to complex integrated testing, it simplifies all testing requirements such as functional testing, regression, end-to-end testing and more. We will create a TestNG xml file and configure our tests.

Chapter 8 will cover Apache Maven, which is a software project management and comprehension tool. Based on the concept of a project object model (POM), Maven can manage a project's build, reporting and documentation from a central piece of information.

Chapter 9 will show us one can execute a Maven Project from Eclipse IDE and later externalize the execution process from command line. This is required because we will be integrating the Maven build in Jenkins.

Chapter 10 will cover the configuration of POM.xml to execute the TestNG xml which will eventually run our Cucumber tests. The POM.xml will be the single execution engine for our framework. We will see how to execute the TestNG xml from Maven's POM.xml.

Chapter 11 will be configuring the Cucumber Reporter in the runner class and generate reports with statistics for our framework.

Chapter 12 will show how we can configure graphical extent reports for our project using Extent Reports, which gives more insight on the test execution status.

Chapter 13 will cover the execution of Cucumber features parallelly using TestNG XML and the ThreadLocal class of Java. Parallel execution speeds up the overall test execution thus reducing time for test completion

Chapter 14 will first cover Jenkins and then we will be integrating the framework with Jenkins and doing configurations for auto trigger.

Downloading the code bundle and coloured images:

Please follow the link to download the
Code Bundle and the *Coloured Images* of the book:

https://rebrand.ly/w2w6ia1

Errata

We take immense pride in our work at BPB Publications and follow best practices to ensure the accuracy of our content to provide with an indulging reading experience to our subscribers. Our readers are our mirrors, and we use their inputs to reflect and improve upon human errors, if any, that may have occurred during the publishing processes involved. To let us maintain the quality and help us reach out to any readers who might be having difficulties due to any unforeseen errors, please write to us at :

errata@bpbonline.com

Your support, suggestions and feedbacks are highly appreciated by the BPB Publications' Family.

BPB is searching for authors like you

If you're interested in becoming an author for BPB, please visit **www.bpbonline.com** and apply today. We have worked with thousands of developers and tech professionals, just like you, to help them share their insight with the global tech community. You can make a general application, apply for a specific hot topic that we are recruiting an author for, or submit your own idea.

The code bundle for the book is also hosted on GitHub at **https://github.com/bpbpublications/Mastering-Behavior-Driven-Development-Using-Cucumber**. In case there's an update to the code, it will be updated on the existing GitHub repository.

We also have other code bundles from our rich catalog of books and videos available at **https://github.com/bpbpublications**. Check them out!

PIRACY

If you come across any illegal copies of our works in any form on the internet, we would be grateful if you would provide us with the location address or website name. Please contact us at **business@bpbonline.com** with a link to the material.

If you are interested in becoming an author

If there is a topic that you have expertise in, and you are interested in either writing or contributing to a book, please visit **www.bpbonline.com**.

REVIEWS

Please leave a review. Once you have read and used this book, why not leave a review on the site that you purchased it from? Potential readers can then see and use your unbiased opinion to make purchase decisions, we at BPB can understand what you think about our products, and our authors can see your feedback on their book. Thank you!

For more information about BPB, please visit **www.bpbonline.com**.

Table of Contents

Chapter 1
Introduction to Behavior Driven Development

Welcome to the exciting world of **Behavior Driven Development** (**BDD**). This book will be divided into three parts. The first part will make the user understand what Cucumber is all about. The second part will explore the Page Object Model and Page Factories. The third part will cover integration of Cucumber with the TestNG framework. It is going to be a very exciting journey, so let's get started and understand what BDD is all about.

BDD helps to bridge the gap between business people and technical people by implementing a language called *'Gherkin'*. It consists of statements in English predominantly, although other languages are available for this purpose too. A group of Gherkin statements together lists a functional flow. These statements are taken by the Automation developer and converted into code using frameworks like Cucumber, JBehave or Specflow. BDD is quite frequently used in Agile projects for getting quick feedback on code quality after developers check in their code in source code management systems like GitHub or SVN. The BDD tests can be configured to execute immediately after the code is checked in.

This chapter will predominantly focus on

- Test Driven Development
- Behavior Driven Development
- Understanding Gherkin

- Introduction to Cucumber
- Understanding the DRY principle
- Components of Cucumber
- Setup of the project in Eclipse
- Setup of TestNG in Eclipse
- Understanding the project structure

Objective

After reading this chapter, the reader will be conversant with the concepts of TDD, BDD, Gherkin and able to create a basic file called '`Feature File`' in the Gherkin Language. He will also learn how the Gherkin file relates to the Step Definition file which is one of the components of Cucumber. He will get knowledge of the project structure and understand how to set up a project in Eclipse along with *TestNG* Plugin integration. This chapter will serve as the foundation for one who wishes to work as a Test Automation Engineer and wants to make a career in BDD framework.

1.1 What is TDD?

TDD stands for Test Driven Development. Test Driven Development is a software development process where test cases are written first taking into consideration the requirements in a traditional project or the user stories in a scrum or agile project. Once the tests are created, minimal code to make the tests pass is created. As and when new tests are created, the code is updated to make the new tests pass and at the same time ensuring that the existing tests pass as well.

TDD (We will refer to this acronym for Test Driven Development going forward) was developed or rediscovered by *Kent Beck* in 2003 to facilitate simple designs. TDD is related to test first programming concepts of Extreme Programming.

1.1.1 Steps involved in a TDD

The steps mentioned below should be followed in a typical Test Driven Development approach.

1. **Write the test**: This activity can be done by the tester or developer where a test is created from the user story, requirement or use case. This is contrasted to the traditional approach of writing unit tests after the code is written. TDD enables the developer to focus on the requirements (We will refer to user stories, traditional requirements or use cases as requirements going forward) before getting started with the code. This differentiated TDD from a traditional development approach.

2. **Run the test to check that it fails**: Prepare the development system such that bare minimum code is there to make your application run like creating the main method or a screen with the required stubs for the database or web service for example. Since writing the test was the very first activity done, it should definitely fail since we don't have any code in place to support the test. If the test fails, then we are sure that the test has been written correctly.

3. **Write the development code**: Now it's time to make our test pass by writing only the required code to make the test pass. It is strongly recommended not to write more code in this step. Writing more code results in what is called **Gold Plating** where you are just giving additional features that are not required at the present moment.

4. **Check to see that the test passes**: Run our first test again and this time it should pass. This helps to ensure that all the correct development code is in place and we can move on to the next test.

5. **Refactor the code**: In the iterative TDD process, we need to make sure that we have not introduced any duplication, all the design principles are met and the methods are where they are supposed to be, that is, logically grouped together in a class.

6. **Repeat with new tests**: Next we write new tests for new requirements and repeat steps 1-5 to ensure that the correct code is written and only the required code is written. TDD will help you build a near defect free application using the minimum amount of code. There are many tools in the market for TDD one of them being JUnit. Since this book is focussed on BDD, we won't go into details about testing with JUnit.

1.2 What is BDD?

BDD is an extension of TDD that makes use of a simple, **Domain Specific Language** (**DSL**). The DSL is in plain English and convert natural language statements into executable tests. The DSL that we are going to study in this book is known by the name Gherkin. The term Gherkin however is specific to Cucumber, JBehave, Behave and Behat software tools.

BDD focuses on:

- Where to start
- What to test and what to exclude
- How much to test
- What to name the tests
- Understanding why a test fails

Let's get our hands dirty with the first DSL in Gherkin.

```
Feature: Cash withdrawal from ATM
Scenario: Successful cash withdrawal
        Given the account balance is $100
        And the card is valid
        And the ATM contains sufficient money
        When the account holder requests $20
        Then the cashslot should dispense $20
        And the account balance should be $80
        And the card should be returned
```

These very simple English statements can be split into three distinct sections.

1) Context: This defines the starting state

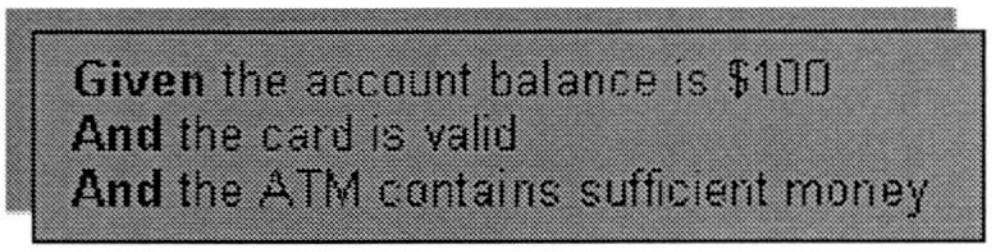

Given the account balance is $100
And the card is valid
And the ATM contains sufficient money

Figure 1.1: *Example of Given keyword*

2) Event: This defines the user's action or actions

When the account holder requests $20

Figure 1.2: *Example of When keyword*

3) Outcomes: This defines the expected results

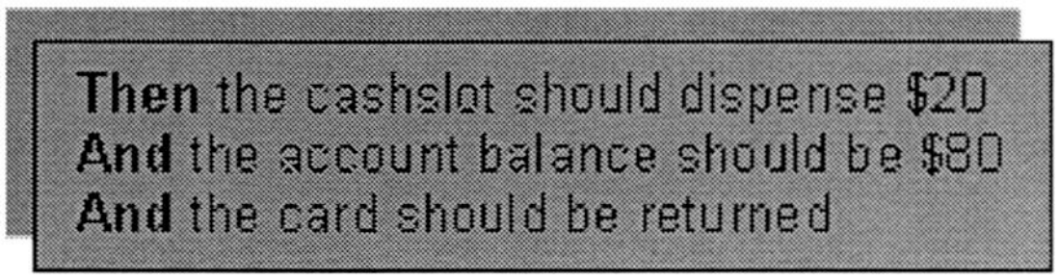

Then the cashslot should dispense $20
And the account balance should be $80
And the card should be returned

Figure 1.3: *Example of 'Then' and 'And' keywords*

The words highlighted in Bold like ''''''"Given", "When", "Then" and ''"And" are known as *Cucumber steps*.

Let's have a look at each of these keywords

1) **Given**: The purpose of Given is to put the system in a known state before the user starts interacting with the system.
2) **When**: The purpose of When steps is to describe the key action the user performs.

3) **Then**: The purpose of Then steps is to observe outcomes. The observations should be related in some way to the business value in your feature description. The observations should also be on some kind of output – that is values that come out of the system.

4) **And**: Used to connect multiple Given, When and Then steps.

The above Domain Specific Language has the Feature and Scenario steps also. We will cover each of these steps in detail when we start designing the Page Object Model Framework. We are now ready to get introduced to Cucumber.

1.3 What is Cucumber?

Cucumber is a tool based on the BDD Framework. Cucumber makes use of Gherkin keywords. Gherkin is a DSL which is used in Cucumber to create test cases. Rather than building linear pieces of code, it is best to understand Cucumber by building a framework of some sort. The framework that can be used for Cucumber is '*The Page Object Model*' which is based on the Page Object Design Pattern. We will understand the Page Object Pattern throughout this book, but let's understand how Cucumber is structured and once we understand that, we will go deeper into understanding how Cucumber fits into the Page Object Model Framework. To get a feel of Cucumber, you may visit **www.cucumber.io** which gives much detail about Cucumber.

1.3.1 Structure of Cucumber

Cucumber comprises three components viz. Runner class, Feature Files and Step Definition classes. Ideally in a scenario where you have no framework, these are all the components you need to execute Cucumber feature file scenarios. Generally, projects are implemented using Frameworks and in the case of Page Object Model Framework, apart from the three mandatory components mentioned above, we have another set called *Page Object classes*. These are Java classes with each page in the **Application Under Test** (**AUT**) corresponding to one Page object class. Thus there is one to one correspondence between Page Objects and Pages in the AUT. When we start designing page objects, we will see how to utilize the concept of inheritance to keep code clean and to avoid code duplication. A very important principle exists known as **Don't Repeat Yourself** (**DRY**) which we will see next. Generally, the default language for the Test Runner class is JUNIT but in this book we will see how to use TestNG for driving the framework. Just because we will use TestNG, we will also make use of TestNG xml to drive the framework. For creating Test Suites in Cucumber, we will make use of something called **Tags**. Using Tags proves to be extremely helpful while working with test suites.

1.4 Understanding the DRY principle

'DRY' simply means Don't Repeat Yourself. What this means is that we write the methods pertaining to web elements on a web page in one class. These methods can pertain to clicking a button or entering values in a test box. To be precise, that one class will have as many methods as there are web elements.

So rather

We would write something like the code line shown below in the class which corresponds to the webpage. Suppose we are dealing with the login page and there is a button with id as 'Login'

```
WebElement btnLogin = driver.findElement(By.id('Login'));

clickLogin(btnLogin);
```

This is always better than doing something like this everywhere in your tests where the Login page is involved.

```
Driver.findElement(By.id('Login')).click();
```

The hard coded value can be replaced by dynamic or static locators which we will see when we look at Page Objects.

1.5 Components of Cucumber Framework

As every other framework, Cucumber also has well defined components. Cucumber has three main components which are Runner class, Feature Files and Step Definition files. Apart from these basic components, we will be using **`testng.xml`**, Maven and Jenkins. We will learn about **`testng.xml`**, Maven and Jenkins in subsequent chapters but now we mainly focus on the three main components which are Runner class, Feature Files, and Step Definition files.

1.5.1 Runner class

This is the class that triggers the framework. The components of the class are given as follows:

1) **CucumberOptions**: This is used on top of the Runner class and helps in specifying where our Feature files, Step Definition files, plugins for report generation like Pretty (for HTML reports), JSON or Rerun.

2) **TestNGCucumberRunner variable**: We create a reference to this class called **`TestNGCucumberRunner`** inside the **`TestRunner`** class. We create a new instance of **`TesrNGCucumberRunner`** passing the parameter as "**`this.getClass`**" inside a method annotated with **`@BeforeClass`**. Similar to **`@BeforeClass`**, we will have a teardown method with **`@AfterClass`** annotation

where we will invoke the **finish()** method on the **TesrNGCucumberRunner** instance.

3) **Methods with @Test annotation**: We can also have test methods that can optionally take data from a data provider. Assigning of groups can also be done for the test methods.

4) **DataProvider Methods**: DataProvider methods with the **@DataProvider** annotation can be designed which can pull data from the data tables present in the feature files.

1.5.2 Feature Files

Feature files are our test cases in simple words. These test cases can be designed by anyone in the team and are in simple English language. The extension of Feature files is **.feature**. The language used in the feature file is called *Gherkin* which is English like and contains keywords like 'GIVEN','WHEN', 'THEN', 'OR', 'BUT', and so on. We have already seen the structure of feature files earlier in this chapter. *Chapter 2, Understanding Feature Files* is dedicated to Feature files.

1.5.3 Step Definition Files

These are '**.java**' files that get generated for us with dummy methods when we run the feature file by right clicking on the feature file in Eclipse and clicking '**Run As Cucumber Feature**'. The dummy step definition methods look like this:

```
@Given("^User is on the home page$")
Public void user_is_on_the_home_page() throws Throwable {
            Throw new PendingException();
}
```

The user has to add code at the place where it says '**Throw new PendingException();**'. The name of the method is immaterial. The methods will be executed based on the match of the regular expression with that of the feature file. So in this case, there should be a Gherkin keyword 'GIVEN' in the feature file followed by "*User is on the home page*". *Chapter 3, Step Definitions* is dedicated to Step Definition files.

Apart from these three components, there might be Java classes that act as page objects. There has to be one java class for each screen or page.

Next, lets learn about Design Patterns that we will implement in this book.

1.6 Design pattern

This book has been written based on the Page Factory Design Pattern. Page Factory Design Pattern optimizes the Page Object Model pattern. In Page Factory pattern, we use **@FindBy** keyword and **initElements** method. We will see how to use this pattern in action in *Chapter 6: Learning about the Page Object Model using Page Factory.*

1.7 Driving the Framework

This framework will be driven using Maven which in turn invokes an xml file called **testng.xml**. **testng.xml** is part of the TestNG framework, which we will study in *Chapter 7, Configuring the TestNG Framework. Chapter 10, Configuring POM.xml to trigger TestNG.xml* will explore how to invoke **testng.xml** from Maven.

1.8 Configuring a Maven Project in Eclipse

We shall use Eclipse IDE in this book. Open the Eclipse IDE and click **File | New | Maven Project** or **File | New | Other | Maven** | Maven Project. The window shown below appears. Select the checkbox '**Create a simple project (Skip archetype selection)**' and click **Next.**

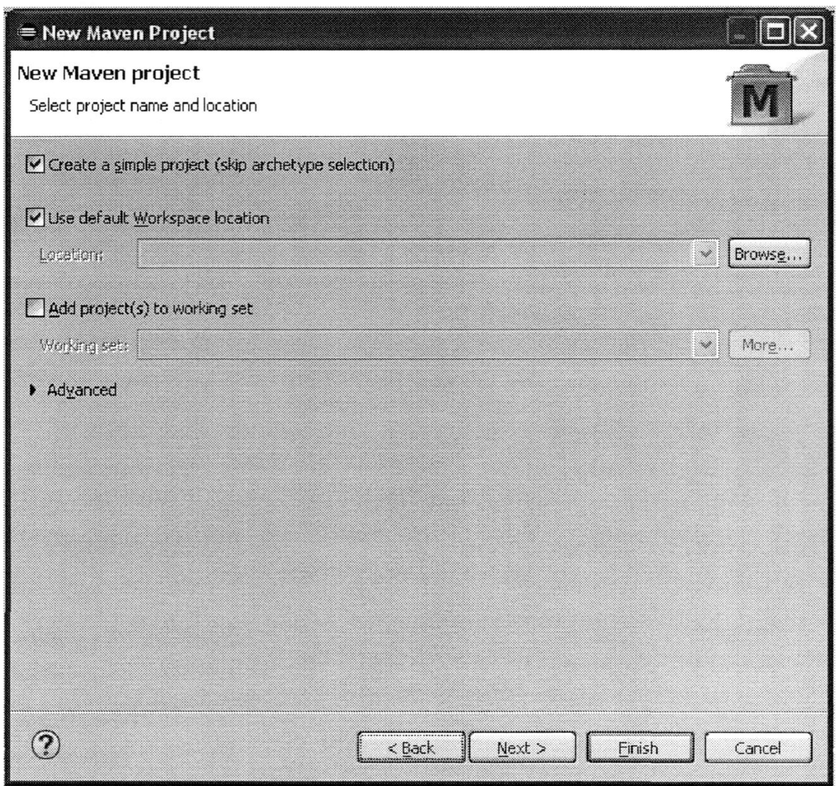

***Figure 1.4:** Creating a new Maven Project*

On the page that appears, enter the details as shown below. An artifact is a file, usually a JAR file that gets deployed to a Maven repository. A Maven build usually produces one or more artifacts, which are files such as a compiled JAR and a "sources" JAR. Each artifact has the following components: group ID (usually a domain name in reverse, like **`com.example.myproject`**), an artifact ID (name of the JAR), and a version string. The word 'SNAPSHOT' in the version indicates that this is a work in progress. The three together identify the artifact uniquely.

A project's dependencies are specified as various artifacts. The snapshot shown below has sample values entered.

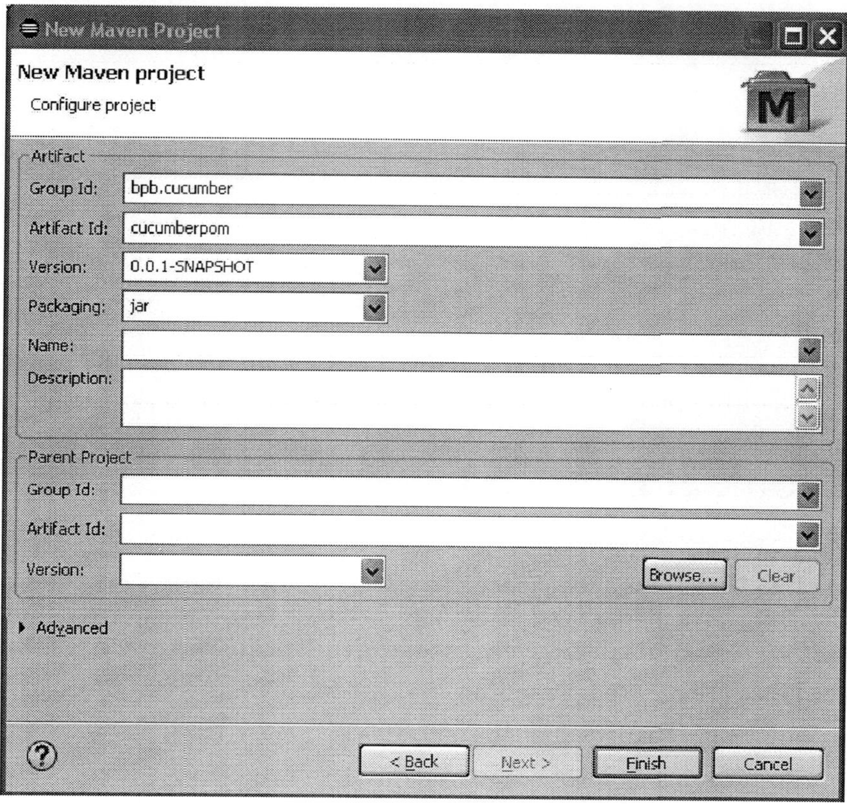

Figure 1.5: Configuring the Maven Project

Click **Finish**. The project gets created as shown as follows:

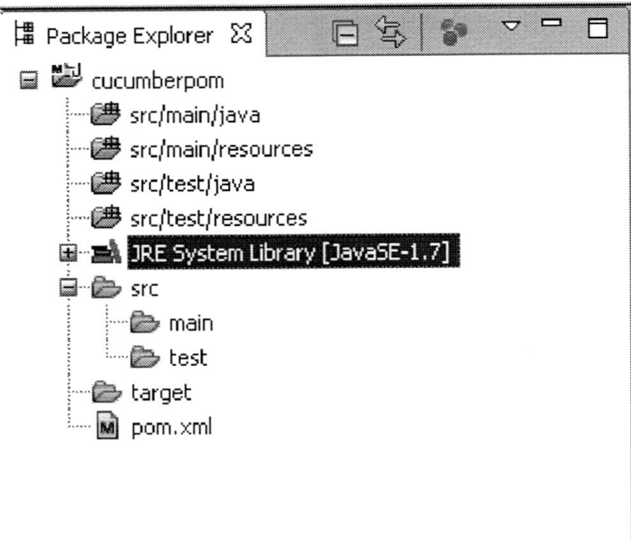

Figure 1.6: Package Explorer

Notice that there is a file called **pom.xml** in the snapshot above. This is where we will mention all our dependencies. We will have a look at the **pom.xml** contents next.

1.8.1 A look at pom.xml

The following code shown shows the **pom.xml** file:

```
<project xmlns="http://maven.apache.org/POM/4.0.0" xmlns:xsi="http://
www.w3.org/2001/XMLSchema-instance" xsi:schemaLocation="http://maven.
apache.org/POM/4.0.0 http://maven.apache.org/xsd/maven-4.0.0.xsd">
  <modelVersion>4.0.0</modelVersion>
  <groupId>org.cucumberbook.pageobjectmodel</groupId>
  <artifactId>cucumberpageobjectmodel</artifactId>
  <version>0.0.1-SNAPSHOT</version>
 <dependencies>
     <dependency>
     <groupId>io.cucumber</groupId>
     <artifactId>cucumber-java</artifactId>
     <version>6.10.4</version>
     </dependency>
```

```
        <dependency>
        <groupId>io.cucumber</groupId>
         <artifactId>cucumber-testng</artifactId>
         <version>6.10.4</version>
         </dependency>

<!-- https://mvnrepository.com/artifact/org.seleniumhq.selenium/
selenium-java -->
       <dependency>
         <groupId>org.seleniumhq.selenium</groupId>
         <artifactId>selenium-java</artifactId>
         <version>3.13.0</version>
     </dependency>

<!-- https://mvnrepository.com/artifact/net.masterthought/cucumber-
reporting -->
     <dependency>
         <groupId>net.masterthought</groupId>
         <artifactId>cucumber-reporting</artifactId>
         <version>4.2.3</version>
    </dependency>
  </dependencies>

</project>
```

Once '**Save**' is clicked there will be some activity in Eclipse and eventually a folder called **Maven Dependencies** will get created which will have the required JAR files.

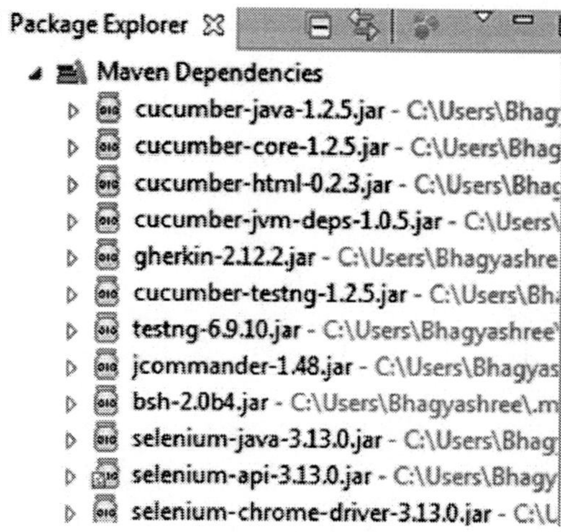

Figure 1.7: Maven Dependencies

This completes the basic setup for starting on our Cucumber project.

1.9 Installing TestNG in Eclipse

We will be using TestNG as our framework in this book and for that we need to install TestNG in Eclipse.

Go to **`Help | Eclipse Marketplace`**. In the Find section, enter **`testng`**. Go to TestNG for Eclipse and click on **`Install`**. The TestNG plugin will get installed in Eclipse.

After installing TestNG, right click on the project and select **`TestNG|Convert to TestNG`**. A **`TestNG.xml`** file will get created at the location of the project.

With this configuration, we are set to start coding. But wait what if your company has a firewall that does not allow you to download files from the internet. For such situations, there is the option of manually adding the required JARs to the build path.

Follow the following steps to configure the Build path:

1. Create a Java project in Eclipse.
2. Right click on the project in Project Explorer.
3. Select **`Build Path | Configure Build Path`**.
4. Click on **`Add External JARs`** and add the required JARs

Next let's move on to the structure of our framework.

1.10 Structure of the Framework

The framework will have a very simple structure as shown as follows:

1) **`src.main.java`** will have packages called **page objects** and **helper classes**
2) **`src.test.resources`** will have folder called **feature files**
3) **`src.test.java`** will have a folder called **step definitions** and that's all to start with. We will be adding more packages as and when needed.

With this we complete the introductory chapter on Selenium WebDriver. In the next chapter, we get introduced to the concept of instantiating a WebDriver object and the various WebDrivers available.

Conclusion

This was the introductory chapter where we got introduced to what Test Driven Development and Behavior Driven Development is. We got introduced to Cucumber as a BDD tool and explored the components of Cucumber like feature files and Step Definition files. We have seen how to setup a Maven project and TestNG in Eclipse. Eventually we saw how our framework would be structured.

In the next chapter, we will see what Feature files are. We will look at each and every component of a Feature file. We will start from a simple Feature and move to complex ones.

Questions

1. Explain what a BDD framework is and various BDD frameworks available in the market.
2. Explain how TDD differs from BDD.
3. Write logic in plain English for logging in to gmail using Gherkin.
4. Explain difference between **Given**, **When**, **And Then**.
5. Explain what a Design Pattern is .

CHAPTER 2
Understanding Feature Files

We will begin by understanding the components of the Cucumber framework in this chapter with the first component which is feature files. Feature files are mostly written in plain English but can be written in other supported languages. They specify a business requirement, for example, logging into a web application and verifying whether the title is correct. This business requirement is specified as a sequence of steps which instruct the system of what action has to be taken in order to fulfil the business requirement.

We will thoroughly understand the different components of a feature file. We will start from a basic feature with one scenario and later build multiple scenarios with different steps using Gherkin keywords like Given, When, Then, And, But, and so on. The reader will understand how easy it is to learn Cucumber feature files and can start developing complex feature files.

This chapter will predominantly focus on:

- Feature files
- Creating feature files
- Plug-in for Feature files
- Introducing feature, Scenario, and Scenario outline
- Understanding the different keywords

- Reusing the same step with different arguments
- Using complex data types
- Understanding DocStrings
- Background step
- Feature file in a different language
- Designing complex feature files
- Introducing Tags

Objectives

After reading this chapter, the reader will be able to:

- Create complex feature files.
- Understand the concepts of Scenario and Scenario outline.
- Learn how to pass arguments in steps.
- Understand the usage of complex data types.
- Grasp the concepts of feature files using examples

2.1 What are feature files?

Feature files are files that have tests written in a descriptive language like English. It is the entry point for the Cucumber framework. Of course, to execute our tests from Jenkins, we will put **`POM.xml`**, a **`testNG.xml`** and a Runner class with cucumber tags. This will form a layer over the feature file.

The following is a sample feature file to log in to the freecrm website:

```
Feature: To test login functionality to www.freecrm.com
      Scenario: To test a successful login
      Given  User navigates to the login page
             When  User enters "admin" as username
             And   User enters "admin" as password
             And   User clicks the Login button
             Then User should be shown User Name on top left corner
```

A feature file contains certain in-built keywords like 'Feature', 'Scenario', 'Given', 'When', 'And', 'But', 'Then', and so on. These are keywords defined in a language known as Gherkin. Gherkin has more keywords apart from the ones shown here, but we will go with the ones mentioned here and understand what each keyword does.

2.1.1 Creating feature files in IDE

Open Eclipse IDE and under **`src.test.resources`** create a package called '**`featurefiles`**'. In this package, create a file called **`feature1.feature`** and follow the steps shown in *figure 2.1* below. This is how the feature file looks like in the Eclipse IDE, as shown in the following screenshot:

feature1.feature

```
Feature: To test login functionality to www.freecrm.com
          Scenario: To test a successful login
                    Given  User navigates to the login page
                    When  User enters "admin" as username
                    And   User enters "admin" as password
                    And   User clicks the Login button
                    Then User should be shown User Name on top left corner
```

Figure 2.1: Feature file in Eclipse IDE

Note that, for a person new to Cucumber, it might be difficult to understand the contents of a feature file at one go.

2.1.1.1 Cucumber Eclipse plugin

In order to make things simpler, a plugin called *'Cucumber Eclipse Plugin'* is required to be installed in Eclipse. Navigate to **`Help | Eclipse Marketplace`** and search for *'Cucumber Eclipse Plugin'*. Install the plugin that appears as shown in the following screenshot. After clicking on the **`Install`** button, accept the license agreement and trigger the installation process. Once the plugin installation is complete, restart the Eclipse IDE:

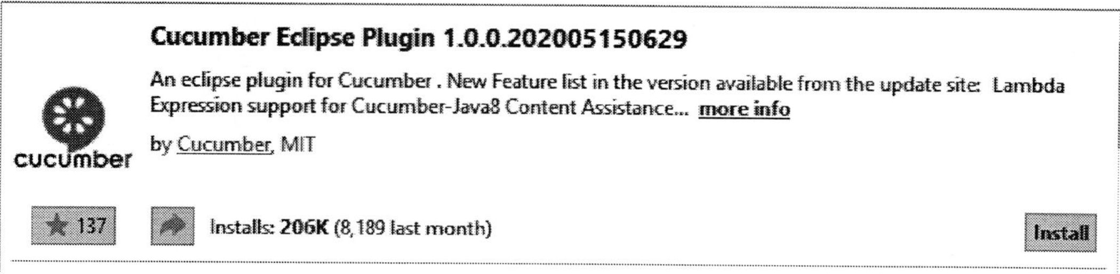

Figure 2.2: Eclipse plugin

Once Eclipse is restarted, note that the appearance of the feature file changes, as shown in the following screenshot:

Figure 2.3: Changes in appearance of the feature file

If a new feature is created, the feature gets created with documentation and the sample steps get created automatically as shown in the following screenshot. The keywords are highlighted in the IDE for ease of understanding.

```
#Author: your.email@your.domain.com
#Keywords Summary :
#Feature: List of scenarios.
#Scenario: Business rule through list of steps with arguments.
#Given: Some precondition step
#When: Some key actions
#Then: To observe outcomes or validation
#And,But: To enumerate more Given,When,Then steps
#Scenario Outline: List of steps for data-driven as an Examples and
<placeholder>
#Examples: Container for s table
#Background: List of steps run before each of the scenarios
#""" (Doc Strings)
#| (Data Tables)
#@ (Tags/Labels):To group Scenarios
#<> (placeholder)
#""
## (Comments)
#Sample Feature Definition Template
@tag
Feature: Title of your feature
  I want to use this template for my feature file

  @tag1
  Scenario: Title of your scenario
    Given I want to write a step with precondition
```

```
    And some other precondition
    When I complete action
    And some other action
    And yet another action
    Then I validate the outcomes
    And check more outcomes

  @tag2
  Scenario Outline: Title of your scenario outline
    Given I want to write a step with <name>
    When I check for the <value> in step
    Then I verify the <status> in step

    Examples:
      | name  | value | status  |
      | name1 |     5 | success |
      | name2 |     7 | Fail    |
```

2.2 Introducing feature, scenario, and scenario outline

A feature file consists of the following keywords: Feature and Scenario or Scenario outline. Let's understand each keyword in detail.

2.2.1 Feature

In Cucumber, feature files specify business needs or requirements. The title of the feature file immediately follows the feature keyword and is on the same line. Three (optional) text lines may follow the line having the feature keyword and specify the intent of the feature file. Feature files contain Scenario or Scenario Outline.

2.2.2 Scenario

Scenarios are similar to test cases in manual testing. They start with the **Scenario** keyword in a new line (other than the one in which the feature intent is present). The **Scenario Title** follows the Scenario keyword and is on the same line as that of the keyword. The **Intent** of the Scenario is specified by three (optional) lines following the line in which the Scenario keyword is present.

A Scenario consists of steps which make use of keywords like **Given**, **When**, **Then**, **And**, **But**, and so on.

An example of a Scenario is shown as follows:

Feature: To test the login functionality to **www.freecrm.com**

Scenario: To test a successful login:

Given User navigates to the login page

When User enters "`admin`" as username

And User enters "`admin`" as password

And User clicks the `Login` button

Then User should be shown User Name on top left corner

Let's explore Scenario Outline next.

2.2.3 Scenario Outline

Scenario Outline is used to execute the same scenario multiple times with different sets of values. Consider the following two scenarios:

Feature: To test login functionality to **www.freecrm.com**

Scenario: To test a successful login

Given User navigates to the login page

When User enters "`admin`" as username

And User enters "`admin`" as password

And User clicks the `Login` button

Then User should be shown User Name on top left corner

Scenario: To test a successful login

Given User navigates to the login page

When User enters "`superuser`" as username

And User enters "`superuser`" as password

And User clicks the `Login` button

Then User should be shown User Name on top left corner

Notice that the second scenario is a redundant one. To eliminate this redundancy, we make use of Scenario Outline shown as follows. We will have 2 iterations for this feature. One for "**admin**" and the other for "**superuser**".

Feature: To test login functionality to **www.freecrm.com**

Scenario Outline: To test a successful login

Given User navigates to the login page

When User enters "**<userName>**" as username

And User enters "**<password>**" as password

And User clicks the **Login** button

Then User should be shown User Name on top left corner

Examples:

```
| userName      | password      |
| admin         | admin         |
| superuser     | superuser     |
```

We now move on to understand what each keyword (GIVEN, WHEN, THEN, and so on) mean.

2.3 Understanding the different keywords

In this section, we will understand the meaning of the different keywords used in a Scenario.

Given: This keyword establishes the initial state of the Application under Test so that the subsequent steps will perform operations on the AUT. An example of the Given keyword is given as follows:

Given User navigates to the login page

When: This keyword describes the user action. An example of the When keyword is given as follows:

When User enters "<userName>" as username

Then: This keyword describes the expected result. An example of the Then keyword is given as follows:

Then User should be shown User Name on top left corner

And: This keyword is used for statements that add to the previous Step/Steps and represent positive statements.

And User enters "superuser" as password

But: This keyword is used for statements that add to the previous Step/Steps and represent negative statements.

But I should not see "Admin" as the role

2.4 Reusing the same step with different arguments

Suppose we have two scenarios where we need to check different sets of data shown as follows:

Scenario: To test a successful login

Given User navigates to the login page

When User enters "**admin**" as username

And User enters "**admin**" as password

And User clicks the **Login** button

Then User should be shown User Name on top left corner

Scenario: To test a successful login

Given User navigates to the login page

When User enters "**superuser**" as username

And User enters "**superuser**" as password

And User clicks the **Login** button

Then User should be shown User Name on top left corner

When these scenarios are executed, the flow of control passes into a Step Definition file where we will see a method similar to the one as follows:

```
@When("^User enters \"(.*?)\" as username$")
  public void User_enters_as_username(String userName) {
      //print the value of data passed from Feature file
      System.out.println(userName);
  }
```

Output:

```
admin
superuser
```

The \"(.*?)\" in the preceding code is known as a **Regular Expression**. Let's understand each part of this regular expression.

- '*' represents zero or more occurrences of the preceding element.
- '?' represents zero or one occurrences of the preceding element.
- '.' represents a single character except the NewLine character.

We will understand new regular expressions as and when we encounter them.

2.5 Using complex data types

In this section, we will use a table with a step shown as follows. The 'Then' step runs three times with different usernames.

Scenario: To test a successful login

Given User navigates to the login page

Then Verify that following users are able to Login

```
| userName    | password  |
| KamleshP    | xyz       |
| RamK        | abc       |
| MikeP       | mkpe      |
```

The corresponding step definition contains the following method. Here, we make use of the DataTable to pull the step table data into a List of String:

```
@Then("^Verify that following users are able to Login$")
public void verify_that_following_users_are_able_to_Login(DataTable loginDetails){
  //Write the code to handle Data Table
  List<List<String>> loginData = loginDetails.raw();
  System.out.println(loginData.get(1).get(0));
}
```

Output:

```
KamleshP
```

2.6 Understanding DocStrings

Doc Strings are large text paragraphs in the feature file which are enclosed within """ (Three quotes). For example, consider the feature file shown below. Please note that this is just an example. The actual **www.freecrm.com** does not contain this text.

Feature: To test login functionality to **www.freecrm.com**

Scenario Outline: To test a successful login

Given User navigates to the login page

When User enters "`<UserName>`" as username

And User enters "`<Password>`" as password

And User clicks the `Login` button

Then User should be shown this paragraph

"""

Welcome to freecrm, your one stop solution for all your HR needs

"""

We will see how to incorporate the doc strings functionality in Java code when we study about step definition files in the next chapter.

2.7 Background Script

A Background script runs before each scenario and looks as follows:

Background:

Given User navigates to the login page

When User enters "`admin`" as username

And User enters "`admin`" as password

And User clicks the `Login` button

Here, the background step executes before each scenario in a feature file. Let's take the case where the Contact and Deal scenario are in the same feature file.

Feature: To test Contact and Deal creation functionality

Scenario: To test a successful contact creation

Given User navigates to the login page

When User enters "`admin`" as username

And User enters "`admin`" as password

And User clicks the **Login** button

And User creates a new Contact

Then User should be shown Contact Confirmation page

Scenario: To test a successful Deal creation

Given User navigates to the login page

When User enters "`admin`" as username

And User enters "`admin`" as password

And User clicks the **Login** button

And User creates a new Deal

Then User should be shown Deal Confirmation page

Once we add the background step, the feature file would look like the one shown as follows:

Feature: To test Contact and Deal creation functionality

Background:

Given User navigates to the login page

When User enters "`admin`" as username

And User enters "`admin`" as password

And User clicks the **Login** button

Scenario: To test a successful contact creation

Given User creates a new Contact

Then User should be shown Contact Confirmation page

Scenario: To test a successful Deal creation

Given User creates a new Deal

Then User should be shown Deal Confirmation page

When the feature file shown above is executed, the background script runs before each scenario executes and acts as a prerequisite for each scenario in the feature file. We will see this in action when we learn about Step Definition files.

2.8 Feature files in a different language

We work in different Geographies in outsourced projects and not everyone understands feature files written in English. Cucumber supports 40 different languages for its feature file. If we need to create the feature file in a language other than English, we have to do two things

1) Include the header # language: xyz as the first line of the feature file
2) Save the file with UTF-8 encoding.

The following code is a feature file in Norwegian:

```
# language: no
Funksjonalitet: Gjett et ord

  Eksempel: Ordmaker starter et spill
      Når Ordmaker starter et spill
      Så må Ordmaker vente på at Gjetter blir med

  Eksempel: Gjetter blir med
      Gitt at Ordmaker har startet et spill med ordet "bløtt"
      Når Gjetter blir med på Ordmakers spill
      Så må Gjetter gjette et ord på 5 bokstaver
```

2.9 Designing complex feature files

We will utilize the knowledge that we have gained so far and create a feature file with Scenario and Scenario outline

Feature: login Page functionality

In order to test login functionality

As a Registered user

Check user login conditions

Scenario: Positive login flow

Given user is on Application home page

And Log in button is present on screen

When user clicks on **Log** in button

Then user is shown login screen

When user enters "**mikeP**" in username field

And user enters "**123456**" in password field

And user clicks **Log** in button

Then user is on home page

And title of home page is "**FreeCRM-HR Unlimited**"

Scenario Outline: Login failure

Given user is on Application home page

When user clicks on Sign in button

Then user is displayed login screen

When user enters "**<UserName>**" in username field

And user enters "**<Password>**" in password field

And user clicks **Log** in button

Then user gets login failed error message.

Examples:

```
| userName        | Password        |
| incorrect           | 123456            |
| pinakinc            | wrongpwd       |
| wrongusr         | wrongpwd       |
```

Scenario: Existing user Verification

Given user is on Application home page

Then we verify following user exists

```
| userName      | Password             |
| Pinakinc          | test123              |
| tester                | yyy123               |
```

We will take a look at how to work with basic and complex feature files using the Step Definition files in the next chapter, although a small excerpt of a Step Definition file was covered in this chapter.

We now move to the final topic of this chapter which is Tags.

2.10 Understanding Cucumber tags

We can create test suites in Cucumber using what are called **Tags**. Tags are written starting with '@' followed by the tag name shown as follows. If you notice, the **@ Regression** tag applies to the entire feature and **@Smoke**, **@Sanity** and **@Negative** apply to individual Scenarios. For now, just remember this syntax. We will look at executing these when we look at the **TestRunner** class. Moreover, we will also see inheritance in feature files.

```
@Regression

Feature: To test login functionality to www.freecrm.com

        @Smoke

    Scenario: To test a successful login

        Given User navigates to the login page

        When User enters "admin" as username

        And   User enters "admin" as password

        And   User clicks the Login button

        Then User should be shown User Name on top left corner

        @Sanity

    Scenario: To test a unsuccessful login with incorrect username

        Given User navigates to the login page

        When User enters "admin1" as username

          And   User enters "admin" as password

        And   User clicks the Login button

        Then User should be shown the login page

        @Negative

    Scenario: To test a unsuccessful login with incorrect password

        Given User navigates to the login page

        When User enters "admin" as username

        And   User enters "admin1" as password

        And   User clicks the Login button

        Then User should be shown the login page
```

This concludes the chapter on Feature files. We have taken a detailed look at all concepts related to feature files, and we are now ready to see the concept of Glue Code in *Chapter 3, Step Definitions*.

Conclusion

This chapter covered the concept of feature files. We got introduced to what a feature file is. We saw simple and complex feature files. We had a detailed look at concepts like feature, Scenario, Scenario Outline, passing data to steps, handling complex data types using DataTables. We even took a look at what docstrings are.

In the next chapter, we will see what Step Definition files are and how to connect the step definition code with a feature file. We will link the various components of Cucumber chapter by chapter.

Questions

1. Explain what a feature file is and create a simple feature with one scenario.
2. Explain the difference between feature, Scenario, and Scenario Outline.
3. Explain use of 'Examples' keyword.
4. Explain DocStrings.
5. Explain what Tags are with an example.

CHAPTER 3
Step Definitions

We will learn about the second component of Cucumber which is Step Definitions. Step Definition files are the glue code between feature files and Page Object classes. Creating Step Definition files is not an overhead because Cucumber auto generates these files for us. We will use the Step Definition files to pass the control flow from feature files to Page Object classes.

We will understand different components of a Step Definition like '**Capture Groups**' and '**Data Tables**' and learn how to implement DocStrings. We will start from Step Definition for a basic feature with one scenario and later build Step Definitions for multiple scenarios with different steps. The reader will be able to speed up with building Step Definitions for a given feature file after reading this chapter.

This chapter will predominantly focus on:

- Step Definitions
- Auto-generate Step Definitions
- Understanding optional Capture/Non-Capture groups
- Handling string and integer arguments
- Implementing DataTables
- Handling DocStrings

- Handling Scenario Outline Data Tables
- Duplicate Step Definitions
- Cucumber Hooks

Objectives

After reading this chapter, the reader will be able to create Step Definitions which connect to the feature files via regular expressions. He will understand the concepts of designing Step Definitions for Scenario and Scenario outline which consist of a table attached to a step and a Scenario outline table with the "`Examples`" keyword. He will learn how to handle arguments that are passed in steps of a feature file. By grasping the creation of effective Step Definitions, the reader will be able to quickly build automated test cases using just feature files and Step Definitions.

3.1 What are Step Definitions?

Step Definition is also called **Glue code** since it forms the glue between the feature files and JavaPage Object classes. These step definitions are a combination of Java code along with regular expressions.

Here is a sample feature file to log in to the freecrm website. Create a new feature file `BPB_1.feature` in the `featurefiles` folder in `src.test.resources`.

Feature: To test login functionality to **www.freecrm.com**

Scenario: To test a successful login

Given User navigates to the login page

When User enters "`admin`" as username

And User enters "`admin`" as password

And User clicks the `Login` button

Then User should be shown User Name on top left corner

In order for this feature to work, the corresponding glue code should be created. The next section explains how to auto-generate this code in an IDE.

3.1.1 Auto generating the Step Definition code in an IDE

Open Eclipse IDE and go to package called '`featurefiles`'. In this package, create a file called `feature1.feature` and enter the steps shown in section *2.1*. In the Project explorer window of Eclipse, right click on the **Feature file** and select **Run As | Cucumber Feature**. In the console window in Eclipse, the following code gets auto-generated. Note that this is just a template code that is provided by the IDE and each of the methods throws a Pending Exception:

```
@Given("^User navigates to the login page$")
public void user_navigates_to_the_login_page() throws Throwable {
    // Write code here that turns the phrase above into concrete actions
    throw new PendingException();
}

@When("^User enters \"([^\"]*)\" as username$")
public void user_enters_as_username(String arg1) throws Throwable {
    // Write code here that turns the phrase above into concrete actions
    throw new PendingException();
}

@When("^User enters \"([^\"]*)\" as password$")
public void user_enters_as_password(String arg1) throws Throwable {
    // Write code here that turns the phrase above into concrete actions
    throw new PendingException();
}

@When("^User clicks the Login button$")
public void user_clicks_the_Login_button() throws Throwable {
    // Write code here that turns the phrase above into concrete actions
    throw new PendingException();
}

@Then("^User should be shown User Name on top left corner$")
public void user_should_be_shown_User_Name_on_top_left_corner() throws
Throwable {
    // Write code here that turns the phrase above into concrete actions
    throw new PendingException();
}
```

In the stepdefinitions folder, create a Java class called '**BPB_1.java**' and add the preceding code with modifications shown as follows:

```
public class BPB_1 {

	@Given("^User navigates to the login page$")
	public void user_navigates_to_the_login_page() throws Throwable {
		System.out.println("Navigated to Login Page");
	}

	@When("^User enters \"(.*?)\" as username$")
	public void user_enters_admin_as_username(String userName) throws
Throwable {
		System.out.println("UserName is: "+userName);
	}

	@And("^User enters \"(.*?)\" as password$")
	public void user_enters_admin_as_password(String password) throws
Throwable {
		System.out.println("Password is: "+password);
	}

	@And("^User clicks the Login button$")
	public void user_clicks_the_Login_button() throws Throwable {
		System.out.println("Login button clicked");
	}

	@Then("^User should be shown User Name on top left corner$")
	public void user_should_be_shown_User_Name_on_top_left_corner()
throws Throwable {
		System.out.println("UserName verified");
	}
}
```

The output is displayed in the following screenshot:

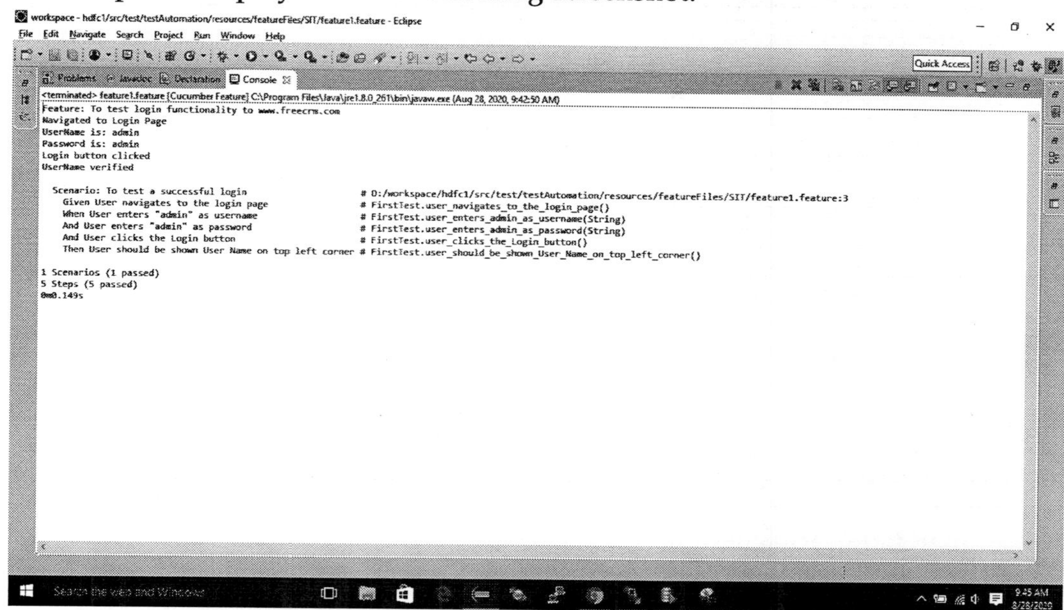

Figure 3.1: Output from the Step definition

Note that the username and password get substituted as '**`admin`**' and the step definition takes this value from the feature file. This value is accepted by a regular expression of the form:

```
@When("^User enters \"(.*?)\" as username$")
```

Here `\"(.*?)\"` is known as a regular expression which is used to pass in arguments from the feature file. Let's understand Capture Groups next.

3.2 Understanding optional Capture/Non-Capture groups

Think about a situation where we have multiple business analysts creating feature files. We will understand '**Capture**' and '**Non-Capture**' groups with an example.

3.2.1 Capture groups

Let's take an example of a step written in two different ways:

```
Given User navigates to the login page.
```

```
Given User goes to the login page.
```

Here, only one word differs in the step which is *'navigates'* and *'goes'*. Apart from that, the step is the same. An efficient step definition shown below takes the action written in the feature file and prints it out. Alter **BPB_1.java** for the code snippet shown as follows:

```
@Given("^User (navigates|goes) to the login page$")
public void user_navigates_to_the_login_page(String entry) throws
Throwable {
        System.out.println("Navigated to Login Page with verb
"+entry);
}
```

The output will look as follows:

With the first '**Given**' step, we get the output shown as follows:

Navigated to Login Page with verb navigates

With the second Given step, we get the output shown as follows:

Navigated to Login Page with verb goes

In the preceding Step Definition, we had to mention an argument for the method. It is not likely that this verb (navigates or goes) will be used anywhere else in the business logic. Here, the verb (navigates or goes) forms a capture group as shown in the regular expression as follows:

```
@Given("^User (navigates|goes) to the login page$")
```

What if we do not want to pass the verb as an argument but still wish to keep the feature files untouched. We need a Non-Capture group in that case.

3.2.2 Non-Capture groups

Consider the same Given step of section *2.2.1*. Non-Capture groups provide the ability to specify different verbs. For example, (navigates | goes) in the feature file without having to pass it as an argument in the Step Definition. The change that needs to be done in **BPB_1.java** in the regular expression of the method in the Step Definition is shown as follows:

```
@Given("^User (?:navigates|goes) to the login page$")
public void user_navigates_to_the_login_page() throws Throwable {
        System.out.println("Navigated to Login Page");
}
```

Output: **Navigated to Login Page** is printed to the console.

The Non-Capture group is mentioned in the regular expression attached to the method with a preceding '?:'. Anything that follows this symbol is considered as a non-capture group, and hence, it need not be passed as an argument to the method as shown above.

3.3 Handling string and integer arguments

We have already seen how to handle String arguments in the few examples given above. Let's take an example of a feature file that contains both String and Integer arguments passed in it. Alter **BPB_1.java** with the contents as follows:

```
Feature: To test login functionality to www.freecrm.com


  Scenario: To test a successful login
    Given User navigates to the login page
    When User enters "admin" as username
   And User enters "admin" as password
   And User enters 12345 as pin
    And User clicks the Login button
    Then User should be shown User Name on top left corner
```

Consider the highlighted steps in bold. The corresponding step definition methods from **BPB_1.java** for those are given as follows:

```
      @And("^User enters \"(.*?)\" as password$")
      public void user_enters_admin_as_password(String password) throws
Throwable {
             System.out.println("Password is: "+password);
      }


      @And("^User enters (\\d+) as pin$")
      public void user_enters_as_password(int pin) throws Throwable {
          // Write code here that turns the phrase above into concrete
actions
             System.out.println("Pin is: "+pin);
      }
```

The output is as follows:

```
Password is: admin
Pin is: 12345
```

Note that the regular expression for an integer argument is specified as (\\d+). The '+' stands for one or more occurrences.

3.4 Implementing Data Tables

In this section, we will see how to implement Scenario DataTables. The following feature file (**BPB_2.feature**) has a Scenario DataTable:

```
Feature: Test for a DataTable

  Scenario: To test a successful login
    Given User navigates to the login page
    Then Verify that following users are able to Login
      | userName | password |
      | KamleshP | xyz      |
      | RamK     | abc      |
      | MikeP    | mkpe     |
```

Create a class **BPB_2.java** and add the code shown as follows:

```
      @Then("^Verify that following users are able to Login$")
      public void verify_that_following_users_are_able_to_
Login(DataTable
                    loginDetails) throws Throwable {
               List<List<String>> loginData = loginDetails.raw();
               for (int i=1;i<loginData.size();i++) {
                    System.out.println("The usernames in the data
table are "+loginData.get(i).get(0));
               }
          }
```

Output:

```
The usernames in the data table are KamleshP
The usernames in the data table are RamK
The usernames in the data table are MikeP
```

DataTables are passed to the Step Definition as the last argument. It is required to import the following in order to make this code to execute:

```
import cucumber.api.DataTable;
import cucumber.api.java.en.And;
import cucumber.api.java.en.Given;
import cucumber.api.java.en.Then;
import cucumber.api.java.en.When;
```

The **`raw()`** method of the DataTable API is used to convert the DataTable into a list of String.

3.5 Handling DocStrings

This is an interesting section in which we will see how to pass a chunk of text to a Step Definition. The chunk of text is called a **DocString**. An example feature (**`BPB_3.feature`**) with DocString is shown as follows:

```
Given a book named "cucumber page object model" by Pinakin Chaubal with
following body
  """
  Title - Cucumber Page Object Model
  Pinakin has written three books on Selenium WebDriver. He loves music
and movies
  """
```

Run this feature by right clicking and selecting **`Run As Cucumber Feature`.** Copy the code for the Step Definition generated by Cucumber and copy it to **`BPB_3.java`** and change it as follows:

```
public class BPB_3 {
      @Given("^a book named \"([^\"]*)\" by Pinakin Chaubal with
following body$")
      public void a_book_named_by_Pinakin_Chaubal_with_following_
body(String bookName, String description) throws Throwable {
            System.out.println("The name of the book is: "+bookName+"
and the detail about the author is: "+description);
      }

}
```

The output is as follows:

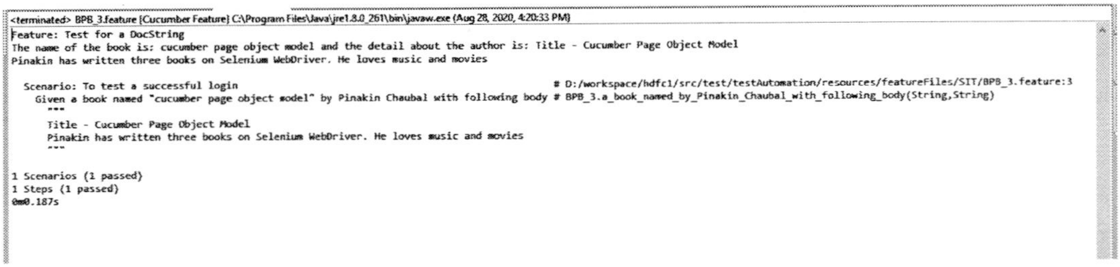

```
<terminated> BPB_3.feature [Cucumber Feature] C:\Program Files\Java\jre1.8.0_261\bin\javaw.exe (Aug 28, 2020, 4:20:33 PM)
Feature: Test for a DocString
The name of the book is: cucumber page object model and the detail about the author is: Title - Cucumber Page Object Model
Pinakin has written three books on Selenium WebDriver. He loves music and movies

  Scenario: To test a successful login                                          # D:/workspace/hdfc1/src/test/testAutomation/resources/featureFiles/SIT/BPB_3.feature:3
    Given a book named "cucumber page object model" by Pinakin Chaubal with following body # BPB_3.a_book_named_by_Pinakin_Chaubal_with_following_body(String,String)
      """
      Title - Cucumber Page Object Model
      Pinakin has written three books on Selenium WebDriver. He loves music and movies
      """

1 Scenarios (1 passed)
1 Steps (1 passed)
0m0.187s
```

Figure 3.2: DocStrings output

The content of the DocString is passed as Argument 2 in the step definition. The DocString in the feature file should be enclosed in three quotes as shown earlier.

3.6 Handling Scenario Outline Data Tables

We will now explore how to handle Scenario Outline Data Tables in Step Definitions.

A feature file (**BPB_4.feature**) with Scenario Outline Data Table is shown as follows:

```
Feature: Test for a DataTable
  Scenario Outline: To test a successful login
    Given User navigates to the login page
    Then Verify that "<userName>" are able to Login to the System

    Examples:
      | userName | password |
      | KamleshP | xyz      |
      | RamK     | abc      |
      | MikeP    | mkpe     |
```

The Step Definition for the feature file is given as follows. Include the following code in **BPB_3.java**:

```
            @Then("^Verify that \"([^\"]*)\" are able to Login to the
System$")
            public void verify_that_are_able_to_Login_to_the_
System(String userName) throws Throwable {
                  System.out.println("UserName: "+userName);;
            }
```

The output is as follows:

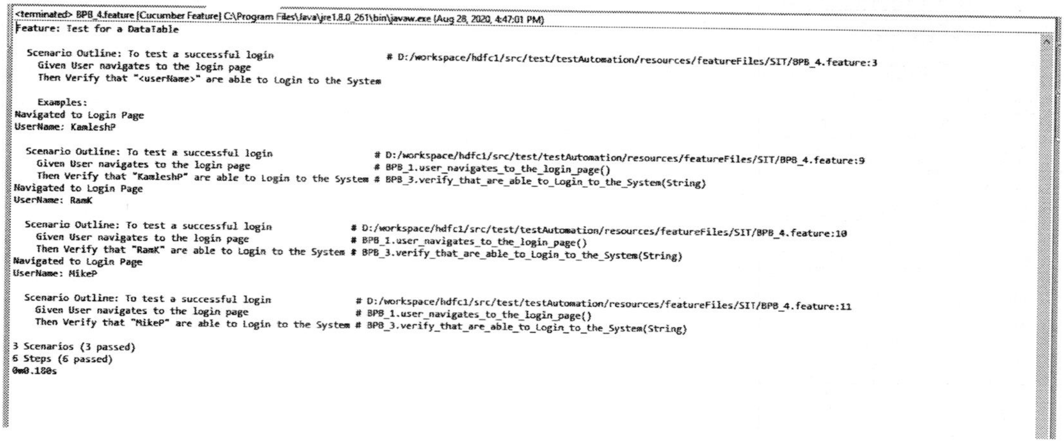

```
<terminated> BPB_4.feature [Cucumber Feature] C:\Program Files\Java\jre1.8.0_261\bin\javaw.exe (Aug 28, 2020, 4:47:01 PM)
Feature: Test for a DataTable

  Scenario Outline: To test a successful login                 # D:/workspace/hdfc1/src/test/testAutomation/resources/featureFiles/SIT/BPB_4.feature:3
    Given User navigates to the login page
    Then Verify that "<userName>" are able to Login to the System

    Examples:
Navigated to Login Page
UserName: KamleshP

  Scenario Outline: To test a successful login                # D:/workspace/hdfc1/src/test/testAutomation/resources/featureFiles/SIT/BPB_4.feature:9
    Given User navigates to the login page                    # BPB_1.user_navigates_to_the_login_page()
    Then Verify that "KamleshP" are able to Login to the System # BPB_3.verify_that_are_able_to_Login_to_the_System(String)
Navigated to Login Page
UserName: RamK

  Scenario Outline: To test a successful login             # D:/workspace/hdfc1/src/test/testAutomation/resources/featureFiles/SIT/BPB_4.feature:10
    Given User navigates to the login page                 # BPB_1.user_navigates_to_the_login_page()
    Then Verify that "RamK" are able to Login to the System # BPB_3.verify_that_are_able_to_Login_to_the_System(String)
Navigated to Login Page
UserName: MikeP

  Scenario Outline: To test a successful login              # D:/workspace/hdfc1/src/test/testAutomation/resources/featureFiles/SIT/BPB_4.feature:11
    Given User navigates to the login page                  # BPB_1.user_navigates_to_the_login_page()
    Then Verify that "MikeP" are able to Login to the System # BPB_3.verify_that_are_able_to_Login_to_the_System(String)

3 Scenarios (3 passed)
6 Steps (6 passed)
0m0.180s
```

Figure 3.3: Scenario outline data tables output

Note: The feature file scans the class path for matching regular expressions. A feature identifies matching glue code based only on the Regular Expression and not on the Method Name. The method name can be changed.

If you notice, there are two sysouts that are displayed. The preceding step definition (**BPB_3.java**) only has one **println** statement and prints the UserName from the Scenario Outline DataTable. The other statement '**Navigated to Login Page**' comes from **BPB_1.java**.

3.7 Duplicate Step Definitions

Let's see what happens when you duplicate a Step Definition method.

Add the following method to **BPB_3.java**:

```
@And("^User (?:navigates|goes) to the login page$")
public void user_navigates_to_the_login_page() throws Throwable {
       System.out.println("Navigated to Login Page");
}
```

With this code introduced, when we run **BPB_4.feature**, we get the '**DuplicateStepDefinitionException**' as shown as follows:

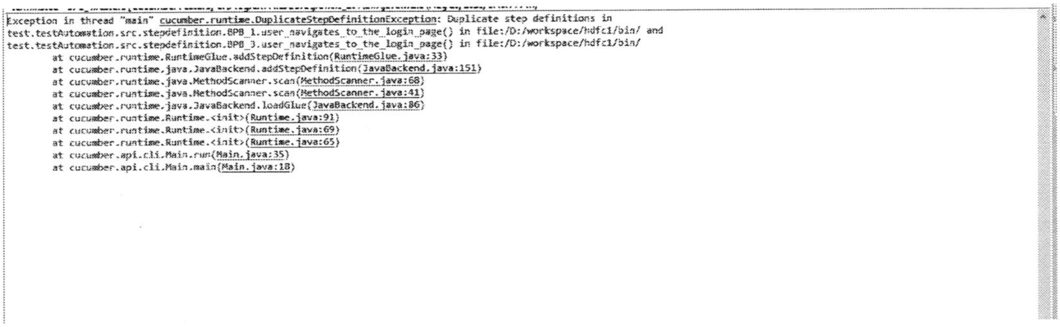

```
Exception in thread "main" cucumber.runtime.DuplicateStepDefinitionException: Duplicate step definitions in
test.testAutomation.src.stepdefinition.BPB_1.user_navigates_to_the_login_page() in file:/D:/workspace/hdfc1/bin/ and
test.testAutomation.src.stepdefinition.BPB_3.user_navigates_to_the_login_page() in file:/D:/workspace/hdfc1/bin/
	at cucumber.runtime.RuntimeGlue.addStepDefinition(RuntimeGlue.java:33)
	at cucumber.runtime.java.JavaBackend.addStepDefinition(JavaBackend.java:151)
	at cucumber.runtime.java.MethodScanner.scan(MethodScanner.java:68)
	at cucumber.runtime.java.MethodScanner.scan(MethodScanner.java:41)
	at cucumber.runtime.java.JavaBackend.loadGlue(JavaBackend.java:86)
	at cucumber.runtime.Runtime.<init>(Runtime.java:91)
	at cucumber.runtime.Runtime.<init>(Runtime.java:69)
	at cucumber.runtime.Runtime.<init>(Runtime.java:65)
	at cucumber.api.cli.Main.run(Main.java:35)
	at cucumber.api.cli.Main.main(Main.java:18)
```

Figure 3.4: *Duplicate Step definitions*

3.8 Cucumber Hooks

Sometimes, we may need to execute actions before and after all the steps of the feature file. This can be implemented using Hooks in Cucumber. Unlike TestNG, Cucumber only supports two hooks which are **@Before** and **@After**. The method annotated by **@Before** gets executed before any step of the feature file is executed and **@After** gets executed after all steps of the feature file are executed. Add the following methods to **BPB_1.java**:

```
@Before
public void setUp() {
	System.out.println("Before  any of the methods");
}


@After
public void tearDown() {
	System.out.println("After all methods");
}
```

Now, try executing **BPB_1.feature** and we get the output as follows:

Output:

```
Before  any of the methods
Navigated to Login Page
UserName is: admin
Password is: admin
```

```
Pin is: 12345
Login button clicked
UserName verified
After all methods
```

This concludes the chapter on Step Definitions. We looked at all concepts related to Step Definitions, and we are now ready to see the concept of Runner classes in *Chapter 4, Learning about the Test Runner*

Conclusion

This chapter covered the concept of Step Definitions. We were introduced to Step Definitions. We saw simple and complex Step Definitions We looked at concepts like Datatables, DocStrings, Scenario Outline, passing data to steps, and handling complex data types using DataTables. We learned how to implement DocStrings.

In the next chapter, we will see what a TestRunner is, and how to connect the Test Runner with the Step definition code and feature files.

Questions

1. Explain what a Step Definition file is.
2. Create a simple feature file and the corresponding Step Definition.
3. Write a Step Definition to implement Data Tables.
4. Write a Step Definition to implement Scenario Outline data tables.
5. Explain what Cucumber Hooks are using a code.

CHAPTER 4
Learning About the Test Runner

In *Chapter 3, Step Definitions,* we learned about the Step Definition component of the Cucumber framework. Steps in the Gherkin language from the Feature file have corresponding code in the Step Definitions. We learned about Step Definitions and how to auto generate the Step Definitions from the Gherkin code in detail. We understood what Capture/Non-Capture groups are. We learned how to handle the string and integer arguments passed in steps. We looked at Data Tables and Scenario Data tables. We learned the concept of DocStrings. We learned what happens when one has duplicate step definitions. Finally, we understood what Cucumber Hooks are.

We will learn about the third component of Cucumber which is the Test Runner. Test Runners are used to execute the features as a test suite. Reporting configurations can be done in the Test Runner. We will make use of annotations to build the Test Runner class. We will start with the Singleton WebDriver class called `singletonDriver.java` to create a single instance of the WebDriver for the entire test. We will make use of specific methods to pull data from Feature files.

We will take a first look at the Selenium code when we design the Singleton Driver. We will learn about the Singleton Pattern when we design the Singleton Driver. We will take a look at the WebDriverManager which will manage the download of the appropriate browser driver for us. Since we have not explored the basic Selenium API methods yet, we will just open and close the driver

Structure

This chapter will predominantly focus on:

- What is the Singleton Pattern?
- Introducing the ThreadLocal class in Java
- Introducing the WebDriverManager library
- Designing a Singleton WebDriver using the WebDriverManager library
- Introducing to the **`GLOBAL_DATA`** class
- Introducing to the **`Test Runner`** class
- Instantiating the Chrome browser instance
- Opening the browser of your choice
- Quitting the driver instance
- Introducing to Tags in TestRunner
- Designing Test Suites with the help of Tags

Objectives

After reading this chapter, the reader will be able to:

- Create Test Runners and specify the location of the feature files and Step Definitions.
- Understand the Singleton Design Pattern in Java.
- Create a Chrome browser instance using the WebDriverManager library.
- Quit the Chrome driver.
- Design Test Suites with the help of Cucumber tags.

4.1 What is the Singleton Pattern?

The single design pattern is one of the creational design patterns in Java. It is used to create an object in Java. Only one instance exists at a given time when the Singleton Pattern is used. Other classes that utilize this class have access to only one instance of this class. The Singleton pattern saves memory since the same instance is utilized time and again.

This pattern is implemented with the use of the components shown as follows:

- **Static member variable**: This holds the instance of the Singleton class. It saves memory as it is static.
- **Private Constructor**: This prevents instantiation of the class from outside using the new keyword.
- **Static Factory method**: This can be accessed using '`ClassName.MethodName`'. This method returns the instance of the Singleton class to the caller.

The Singleton pattern is used in test automation for the WebDriver instance creation. Apart from this in development, it is used in Database and Multi-Threaded applications. It is also used in thread pools, caching, logging, and so on.

We will take a look at how we can make our code thread-safe in the next section.

4.2 Introduction to the ThreadLocal class in Java

We will now take a look at how we can achieve parallel execution in Selenium. We will make use of parallel execution features of TestNG which requires the creation of a separate thread for each driver instance. The ThreadLocal class of Java will be utilized for this purpose. By declaring variables as shown in the following code, we make sure that each thread has its own copy of the WebDriver instance:

```
ThreadLocal<WebDriver> driver = new ThreadLocal<WebDriver>();
```

Apart from the Driver instance, we will have the variables which hold the session ID, Browser name, the platform (Windows or Linux), and the Version:

```
private ThreadLocal<String> sessId = new ThreadLocal<String>();
private ThreadLocal<String> sBrwsr = new ThreadLocal<String>();
private ThreadLocal<String> sPltfrm = new ThreadLocal<String>();
private ThreadLocal<String> sVrsn = new ThreadLocal<String>();
```

Each of these variables is thread-safe. Note that in *section 4.1*, when were introduced to the Singleton pattern which can be used to initiate a single browser session throughout. Here, we make the driver instance thread safe, thus giving an opportunity to launch multiple driver instances. Next, we will take a look at the `WebDriverManager` library which helps us in automating the driver binary management.

4.3 Introducing the WebDriverManager library

Enter the code shown as follows in the Main method:

```
System. setProperty("webdriver.chrome.driver", "path of the exe
file\\chromedriver.exe");

WebDriver driver=new ChromeDriver();
```

This will open a Chrome browser session. The driver executable has to be downloaded manually. This works fine but the problem with this is that every time the Chrome browser gets an update, the version of the driver executable has to be changed. Suppose testing has to be done on a specific version of a browser. This is not possible when we have to download the driver executable manually.

The WebDriverManager library helps us in this by automatic management of the driver executable. WebDriverManager comes as a Maven dependency shown as follows:

```
  <!-- https://mvnrepository.com/artifact/io.github.bonigarcia/
webdrivermanager -->

<dependency>

    <groupId>io.github.bonigarcia</groupId>

    <artifactId>webdrivermanager</artifactId>

    <version>3.6.2</version>

</dependency>
```

Right click on the project and select **Maven | Update Project.**

The following lines

```
System. setProperty("webdriver.chrome.driver", "path of the exe file\\
chromedriver.exe");

WebDriver driver=new ChromeDriver();
```

Will be replaced with the following:

```
WebDriverManager.chromedriver().setup();

WebDriver chromeDriver = new ChromeDriver();
```

Execute this code and you will see a Chrome browser opening with the console output shown as follows:

```
Sep 03, 2020 11:27:59 AM org.openqa.selenium.remote.DesiredCapabilities chrome
INFO: Using `new ChromeOptions()` is preferred to `DesiredCapabilities.chrome()`
SLF4J: Failed to load class "org.slf4j.impl.StaticLoggerBinder".
SLF4J: Defaulting to no-operation (NOP) logger implementation
SLF4J: See http://www.slf4j.org/codes.html#StaticLoggerBinder for further details.
Starting ChromeDriver 83.0.4103.39 (ccbf011cb2d2b19b506d844400483861342c20cd-refs/branch-heads/4103@{#416}) on port 32907
Only local connections are allowed.
Please see https://chromedriver.chromium.org/security-considerations for suggestions on keeping ChromeDriver safe.
ChromeDriver was started successfully.
Sep 03, 2020 11:29:14 AM org.openqa.selenium.remote.ProtocolHandshake createSession
INFO: Detected dialect: W3C
```

Figure 4.1: *WebDriverManager output for Chrome browser*

Next, we will take a look at how to design the Singleton WebDriver class using the **WebDriverManager** library.

4.4 Design a Singleton WebDriver using the WebDriverManager library

Since we have seen concepts such as Singleton pattern, the **ThreadLocal** class, and the **WebDriverManager** library, we can now design the Singleton WebDriver class. Instead of looking at the full code, we will look at the individual methods for ease of understanding. We have already seen the ThreadLocal variables that will be used in this class in *section 4.2*.

4.4.1 Private Constructor

The Singleton WebDriver class will have a private constructor so that this class cannot be instantiated from outside using the **new()** keyword. The constructor is shown as follows:

```
// Private constructor in order to block instantiation of this class
from outside

private SingletonDriver() {

}
```

We now look at how to fetch the Single instance of the SingletonDriver class.

4.4.2 Fetching the Singleton class instance

The next component of the **SingletonDriver** class is the method to fetch the Singleton instance of the driver class so that it can be accessed from outside.

```
/**

           * getInstance method will fetch the active driver instance

           *

           * @return SingletoDriver

 */

 public static SingletonDriver getInstance() {

       if ( instance == null ) {

          instance = new SingletonDriver();

       }

       return instance;

}
```

We will next look at setting the Driver and its preferences with the **setDrvr** method.

4.4.3 Setting the Driver and its preferences

The next component of the **SingletonDriver** class is the method to set the Singleton instance of the driver class to Chrome, Firefox, or Internet Explorer based on the arguments passed to the **setDrvr** method. We will use WebDriverManager to instantiate the drivers. Here, we will also set the browser, platform, and environment to the respective ThreadLocal variables. The code is as follows:

```
 /**
  * setDrvr method to create driver instance
  * Parameters are mentioned below
  * browser
  * environment
  * platform
  * optPreferences
  * also throws Exception
  */
@SafeVarargs
public final void setDrvr(String brwsr,
                            String pltfrm,
                            String envrnmnt,
                            Map<String, Object>... optPrefs)
                            throws Exception {

    DesiredCapabilities caps = null;
    String getPltfrm = null;
    props.load(new FileInputStream(GLOBAL_DATA.SE_PROPRTS));

    switch (brwsr) {
        case "firefox":
            caps = DesiredCapabilities.firefox();

            FirefoxOptions ffOpts = new FirefoxOptions();
            FirefoxProfile ffProfile = new FirefoxProfile();

            ffProfile.setPreference("browser.autofocus",
                                    true);
```

```
                    ffProfile.setPreference("browser.tabs.remote.
autostart.2", false);

                    caps.setCapability(FirefoxDriver.PROFILE,
                                       ffProfile);
                    caps.setCapability("marionette",
                                        true);

                    // then pass them to the local WebDriver
                    if ( envrnmnt.equalsIgnoreCase("local") ) {
                        WebDriverManager.firefoxdriver().setup();
                        webDriver.set(new
                        FirefoxDriver(ffOpts.merge(caps)));
                    }

                    break;
                case "chrome":
                    caps = DesiredCapabilities.chrome();

                    ChromeOptions chOptions = new ChromeOptions();
                    Map<String, Object> chromePrefs =
                        new HashMap<String, Object>();

                    chromePrefs.put("credentials_enable_service",
                                    false);

                    chOptions.setExperimentalOption("prefs",
                                                    chromePrefs);

                    chOptions.addArguments("--disable-plugins",
                                           "--disable-extensions",
                                           "--disable-popup-
blocking");

                    caps.setCapability(ChromeOptions.CAPABILITY,
                                       chOptions);
                    caps.setCapability("applicationCacheEnabled",
                                       false);
```

```
        if ( envrnmnt.equalsIgnoreCase("local") ) {
            WebDriverManager.chromedriver().setup();
            webDriver.set(new
            ChromeDriver(chOptions.merge(caps)));
        }

        break;
    case "internet explorer":
        caps = DesiredCapabilities.internetExplorer();

        InternetExplorerOptions ieOpts =
            new InternetExplorerOptions();

        ieOpts.requireWindowFocus();
        ieOpts.merge(caps);

        caps.setCapability("requireWindowFocus",
                           true);

        if ( envrnmnt.equalsIgnoreCase("local") ) {
            WebDriverManager.iedriver().setup();
            webDriver.set(new InternetExplorerDriver(
                          ieOpts.merge(caps)));
        }

        break;
}

getEnv = envrnmnt;
getPltfrm = pltfrm;

sessId.set(((RemoteWebDriver) webDriver.get())
.getSessionId().toString());

sBrwsr.set(caps.getBrowserName());
sVrsn.set(caps.getVersion());
sPltfrm.set(getPltfrm);
```

```
        System.out.println("\n*** THE TEST ENVIRONMENT DETAILS ARE "
                + getSessBrwsr().toUpperCase()
                + "||" + getSessPltfrm().toUpperCase()
                + "||" + getEnv.toUpperCase()
                + "||Selenium Version is"
                + props.getProperty("selenium.revision")
                + "||Session ID="
                + getSessId()
                + "\n");

        getDrvr().manage().timeouts().implicitlyWait(
            IMPLCT_TIMEOUT, TimeUnit.SECONDS);
        getDrvr().manage().window().maximize();
    }
```

Next, we have a look at fetching the WebDriver instance.

4.4.4 Fetching the WebDriver instance

The following method is used to fetch the active **WebDriver** instance. The method used to fetch the instance is **get()** which is invoked on the WebDriver instance. The code is as follows:

```
/**
     * getDriver method to fetch active driver
     *
     * @return WebDriver
     */
    public WebDriver getDrvr() {
        return webDriver.get();
    }
```

The other preferences can be fetched in a similar fashion. Finally, we have the code to close the browser.

4.4.5 Closing the browser session

Finally, in this section, we will look at closing the browser session by invoking the **quit()** method on the **getDrvr()** method shown as follows:

```
/**
 * closeDriver method to close active driver instance
 *
 */
 public void closeDriver() {
      try {
                 getDrvr().quit();
          }

       catch ( Exception e ) {
        }
 }
```

One more thing to look at is the **GLOBAL_DATA** class where we have defined all our constants.

4.5 Introduction to the GLOBAL_DATA class

Now, since we have our **SingletonDriver** class in place, it is time to see a class that was used in the **SingletonDriver** class. This class is the **GLOBAL_DATA** class which is used specifically for constants. The code is as follows:

```
public class GLOBAL_DATA {
         // constant variables
         public static final String BRWSR = "chrome";
         public static final String PLTFRM = "Windows 10";
         public static final String ENVRNMNT = "local";
         public static String DEFLT_BRWSR = null;
         public static String DEFLT_PLTFRM = null;
         public static String DEFLT_ENVRNMNT = null;
         public static String PROPTS_PATH = null;

         // driver class default values
         public static String propFile = "src/main/resources/selenium.
properties";
         public static final String SE_PROPRTS =
```

```
        new File(propFile).getAbsolutePath();

        // test output path default values
        public static final String TEST_OUTPT_PTH = "testOutput/";
        public static final String LOGFLE_PTH = TEST_OUTPT_PTH +
        "Logs/";
        public static final String REPORT_PTH = TEST_OUTPT_PTH +
        "Reports/";
        public static final String IMAGE_PATH = TEST_OUTPT_PTH +
        "Images/";

        // timeout default values
        public static final int TIMEOUT_MNT = 60;
        public static final int TIMEOUT_SCND = 1;
        public static final int TIMEOUT_ZR = 0;
    }
```

The constant SE_PROPRTS has been accessed in the **SingletonDriver** class using **GLOBAL_DATA.SE_PROPRTS**.

Next, we will move to the main topic of this chapter which is the Test Runner class which we will create using TestNG.

4.6 Introduction to the Test Runner class

The Test Runner is the point in our framework where we have details like the location of the Feature files, Step Definitions, Reporting configurations, and tags. Apart from this, the Test Runner class will extend a class called **AbstractTestNGCucumberTests**. We have a test method for executing the steps in the feature file. In case there is a data table that provides data to the feature, we have a data provider method. We also have a private variable of type private **TestNGCucumberRunner** which is declared as follows:

```
private TestNGCucumberRunner;
```

The steps from the feature file are read by the Data Provider and read by the **CucumberFeatureWrapper** parameter. The **runCucumber** method of the **TestNGCucumberRunner** takes in one argument which has the Feature file data that can be pulled using the **getCucumberFeature()** method.

```
@Test(dataProvider="features")
public void feature(CucumberFeatureWrapper cucumberFeature) {
```

```
        testNGCucumberRunner.runCucumber(cucumberFeature.
getCucumberFeature());
}
```

The following code is our DataProvider which returns a two-dimensional Object Array of the data of the Feature file, including the DataTable data. We will first instantiate an object of **`TestNGCucumberRunner`** if it is null and return the Feature file data using the **`provideFeatures()`** method:

```
@DataProvider
public Object[][] features() {
        if(testNGCucumberRunner == null){
                        testNGCucumberRunner = new
TestNGCucumberRunner(this.getClass());
        }
                return testNGCucumberRunner.provideFeatures();
}
```

The preceding **`feature()`** method is executed for all steps and iterations of every feature. The output is shown in the following screenshot:

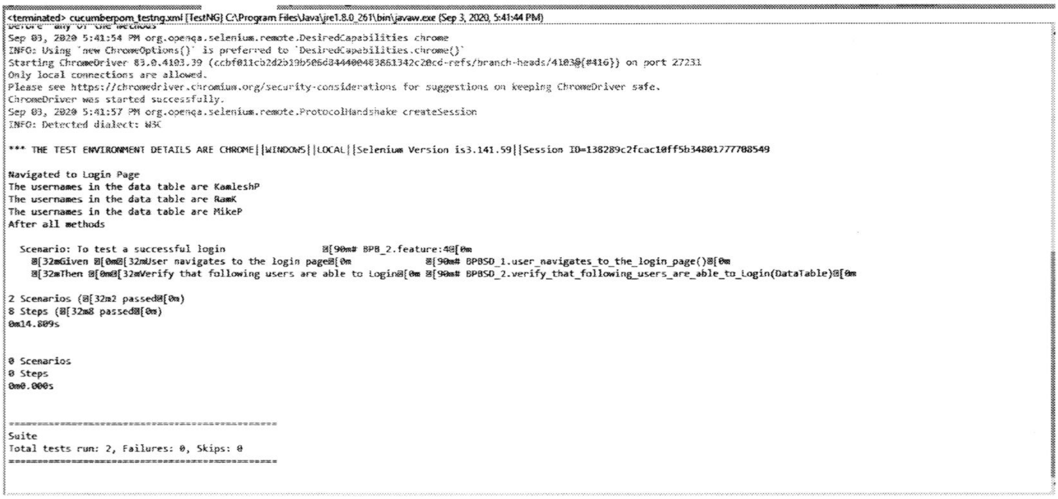

```
<terminated> cucumberpom_testng.xml [TestNG] C:\Program Files\Java\jre1.8.0_261\bin\javaw.exe (Sep 3, 2020, 5:41:44 PM)
Sep 03, 2020 5:41:54 PM org.openqa.selenium.remote.DesiredCapabilities chrome
INFO: Using `new ChromeOptions()` is preferred to `DesiredCapabilities.chrome()`
Starting ChromeDriver 83.0.4103.39 (ccbf011cb2d2b19b506d844400483861342c20cd-refs/branch-heads/4103@{#416}) on port 27231
Only local connections are allowed.
Please see https://chromedriver.chromium.org/security-considerations for suggestions on keeping ChromeDriver safe.
ChromeDriver was started successfully.
Sep 03, 2020 5:41:57 PM org.openqa.selenium.remote.ProtocolHandshake createSession
INFO: Detected dialect: W3C

*** THE TEST ENVIRONMENT DETAILS ARE CHROME||WINDOWS||LOCAL||Selenium Version is3.141.59||Session ID=138289c2fcac10ff5b34801777708549

Navigated to Login Page
The usernames in the data table are KamleshP
The usernames in the data table are RamK
The usernames in the data table are MikeP
After all methods

  Scenario: To test a successful login                 [90m# BPB_2.feature:4[0m
    [32mGiven [0m[32mUser navigates to the login page[0m              [90m# BPBSD_1.user_navigates_to_the_login_page()[0m
    [32mThen [0m[32mVerify that following users are able to Login[0m [90m# BPBSD_2.verify_that_following_users_are_able_to_Login(DataTable)[0m

2 Scenarios ([32m2 passed[0m)
8 Steps ([32m8 passed[0m)
0m14.809s


0 Scenarios
0 Steps
0m0.000s


===============================================
Suite
Total tests run: 2, Failures: 0, Skips: 0
===============================================
```

Figure 4.2: Output of the Test Runner

Apart from the output shown here, browser sessions of Chrome are opened and closed twice since we have two executions for 2 scenarios.

Please Note: To execute this TestRunner class, we will make use of the TestNG xml shown in the following code. We will explore this xml when we learn about TestNG in the upcoming chapters.

```
<?xml version="1.0" encoding="UTF-8"?>
<!DOCTYPE suite SYSTEM "http://testng.org/testng-1.0.dtd">
<suite name="Suite">
  <test thread-count="5" name="Test">
    <classes>
      <class name="testrunner.BPBTR_1"/>
    </classes>
  </test> <!-- Test -->
</suite> <!-- Suite -->
```

Next, let's see where and how we have added the code to open and close the browser after each Feature file execution.

4.7 Instantiating the Chrome browser instance

In order to open a Chrome browser instance, create a Step Definition (**BPBSD_0.java**) with the code shown as follows. Here, we have hard coded the value of the browser, platform, and so on. We will see a better approach in the next section when we modify our feature file to incorporate the browser in our scenarios. We will have the browser passed in the step itself; for example, Open a "*Chrome*" browser or Open a "*Firefox*" browser:

```
public class BPBSD_0 {
	@Before
	public void setUp() {
		System.out.println("Before  any of the methods");
		try {
			SingletonDriver.getInstance().setDrvr(GLOBAL_DATA.
BRWSR, GLOBAL_DATA.PLTFRM, GLOBAL_DATA.ENVRNMNT, null);
		} catch (Exception e) {
			// TODO Auto-generated catch block
			e.printStackTrace();
		}
	}
}
```

Let's now see how we can add a step to open the browser of our choice.

4.8 Opening the browser of your choice

Let's create a feature file (**BPBF_5.feature**) with just one step for opening the browser of our choice. We have explicitly mentioned in the **Given** step which browser to open, on which platform, and whether it will be used with Selenium Grid:

```
@Single
Feature: Open browser of choice
  I want to open browser of my choice
  Scenario: Open browser of choice
    Given I open the "chrome" browser on "windows" and "local"
```

The corresponding Step Definition which invokes the **setDrvr()** method of the **SingletonDriver** class is shown as follows:

```
public class BPBSD_00 {
      @Given("^I open the \"([^\"]*)\" browser on \"([^\"]*)\" and 
\"([^\"]*)\"$")
      public void i_open_the_browser(String browserName, String 
platform, String gridSetting) throws Throwable {
            // Write code here that turns the phrase above into concrete 
actions
                  try {
                        SingletonDriver.getInstance().setDrvr(browserName, 
platform, gridSetting, null);
                  } catch (Exception e) {
                        // TODO Auto-generated catch block
                        e.printStackTrace();
                  }

      }
}
```

Please note that the **@Before** annotation from *section 4.6* should be removed prior to running this code otherwise two Chrome browser sessions will be opened.

4.9 Quitting the driver instance

In order to quit the browser after a Feature file execution, create a Step Definition file BPBSD_99 and write the code as follows:

```
public class BPBSD_99 {
	@After
	public void tearDown() {
		System.out.println("After all methods");
		SingletonDriver.getInstance().closeDriver();


	}
}
```

Here, we get the Singleton instance and then invoke the **closeDriver()** method.

4.10 Introduction to Tags in TestRunner

We might have a collection of multiple scenarios in one Feature file and we also may have multiple Feature files as well. Suppose, we are doing Smoke, Regression, and FilterTest and want to group our scenarios under these, then we have the option of running each group separately. This can be achieved with the help of tags. Tags are written in the Feature file with the syntax shown as follows:

@Smoke

Similarly, if we wish to run test cases corresponding to the **@Smoke** tag, we need to mention this tag in the Test Runner in Cucumber options as indicated shown as follows:

```
@CucumberOptions(features = { "src/test/resources/featurefiles" }, glue =
{ "stepdefinitions" }, plugin = {
		"pretty", "html:target/cucumber" }, tags = {"@Smoke"})
```

Consider the example of a Feature file (**BPBF_6.feature**):

```
#Sample Feature to show tags and tag inheritance
@FunctionalSuite
Feature: Title of your feature
  I want to use this template for my feature file

  @Smoke
```

```
  Scenario: Smoke Test 1
    Given I want to execute "Smoke Test 1" test

  @FilterTest
  Scenario: Filter Test 1
    Given I want to execute "Filter Test 1" test

  @Regression
  Scenario: Regression Test 1
    Given I want to execute "Regression Test 1" test

  @Smoke @FilterTest
  Scenario: Smoke/Filter Test 1
    Given I want to execute "Smoke/Filter Test 1" test

  @Smoke @Regression
  Scenario: Smoke/Regression Test 1
    Given I want to execute "Smoke/Regression" test

  @Regression @FilterTest
  Scenario: Regression/Filter Test 1
    Given I want to execute "Regression/Filter Test 1" test

  Scenario: Generic Test 1
    Given I want to execute "Generic" test
```

The corresponding step definition is shown as follows:

```
public class BPBSD_4 {
        @Given("^I want to execute \"([^\"]*)\" test$")
        public void i_want_to_execute_test(String type) throws Throwable
{
                // Write code here that turns the phrase above into concrete
actions
                System.out.println("This test is of type: "+type);
        }
}
```

If the TestRunner is executed with '`tags = {"@Smoke"}`', then three scenarios get executed as shown in the following screenshot:

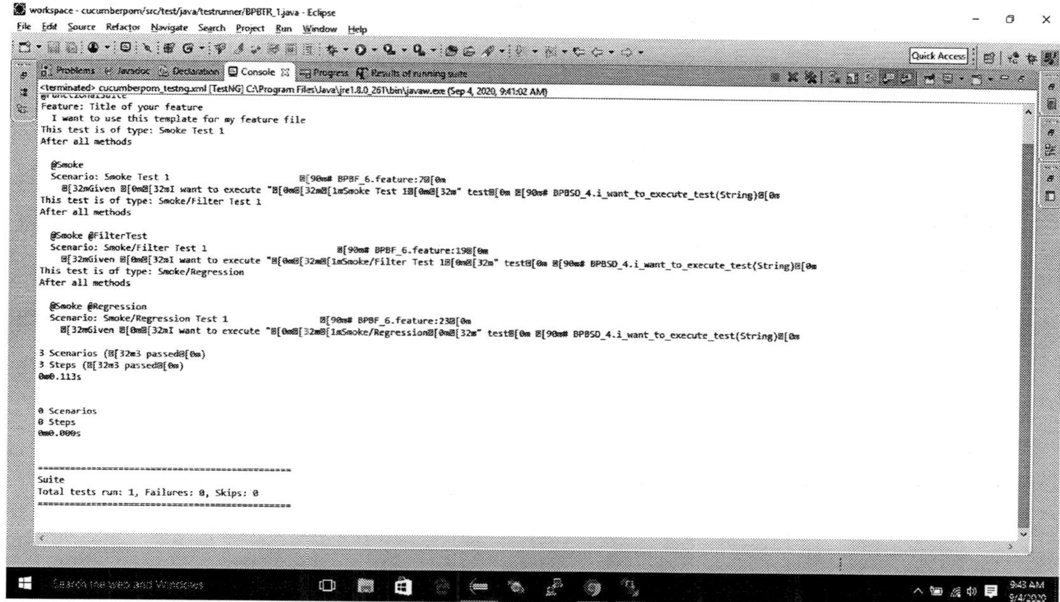

Figure 4.3: Tag execution

Next, we will see how to club two tags so that scenarios which have either of the tags get executed.

4.11 Designing Test Suites with the help of tags

In this section, we will see how to create test suites where we want to execute test cases corresponding to multiple tags. Change the tag to **`tags = {"@FunctionalSuite,@Smoke"}`**. Here, **`@FunctionalSuite`** is a tag attached at the Feature level and **`@Smoke`** is attached to the Scenario level. The preceding tag imposes an '**OR**' condition and executes test cases with either **`@FunctionalSuite`** or **`@Smoke`**. Since

@FunctionalSuite is at the Feature level, it applies to all the scenarios inside the Feature and thus all 7 scenarios are executed as shown in the following screenshot:

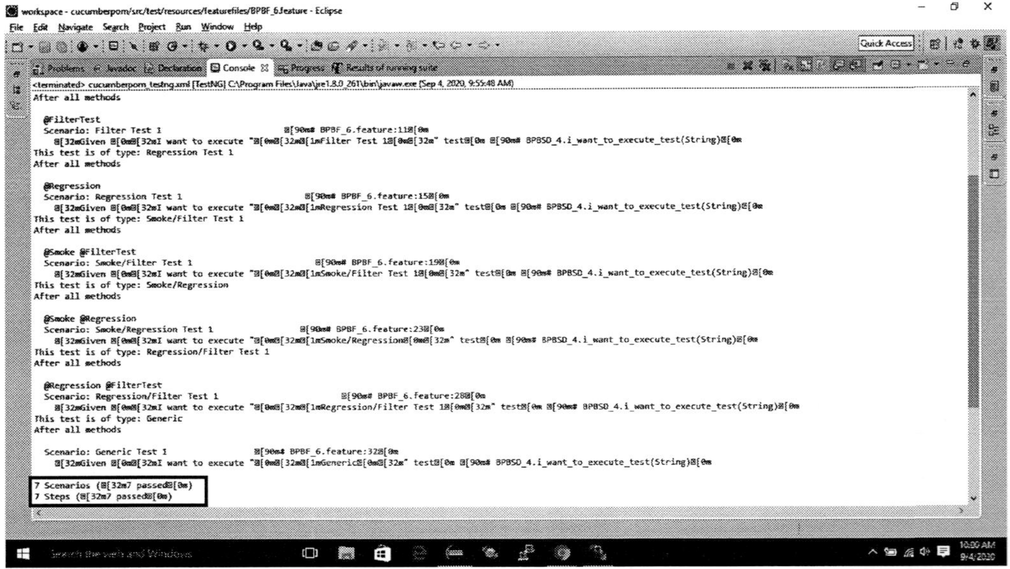

Figure 4.4: clubbing Tags with OR condition

If we wish to impose an 'AND' condition, change the tags as **tags = {"@FunctionalSuite","@Smoke"}**. This will execute all scenarios with tags **@FunctionalSuite** and **@Smoke**. The **@FunctionalSuite** tag applies to all scenarios since it is at the Feature level. There are three scenarios with the **@Smoke** tag. Hence, 3 scenarios are executed as shown in the following screenshot:

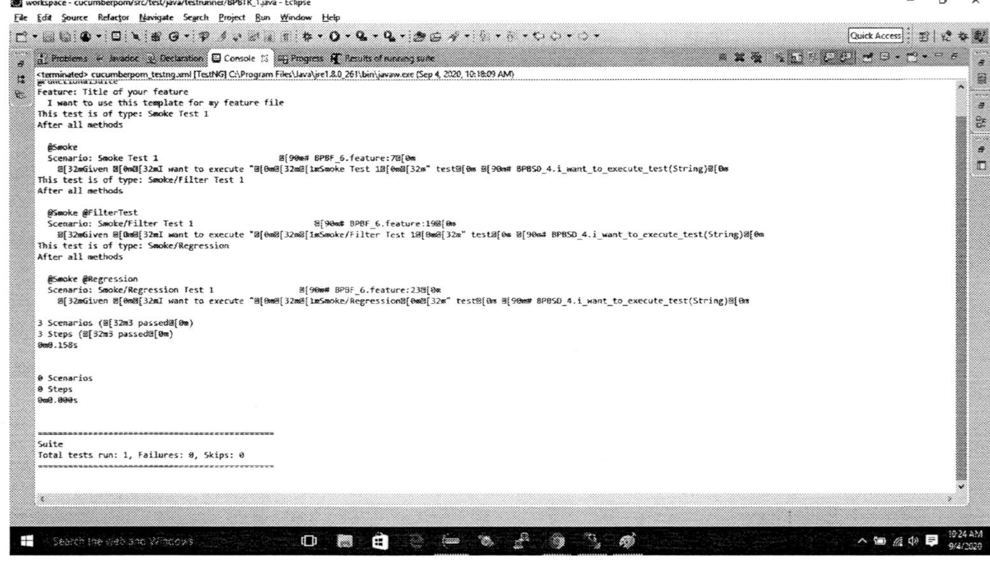

Figure 4.5: Clubbing tags with AND condition

A negation test is also possible. If a '~' is mentioned in the tag, then all scenarios which dont have the **`@Smoke`** tag get executed which is shown as follows:

```
tags = {"@FunctionalSuite","~@Smoke"}
```

The output is shown as follows where 3 scenarios which don't have the **`@Smoke`** tag get executed:

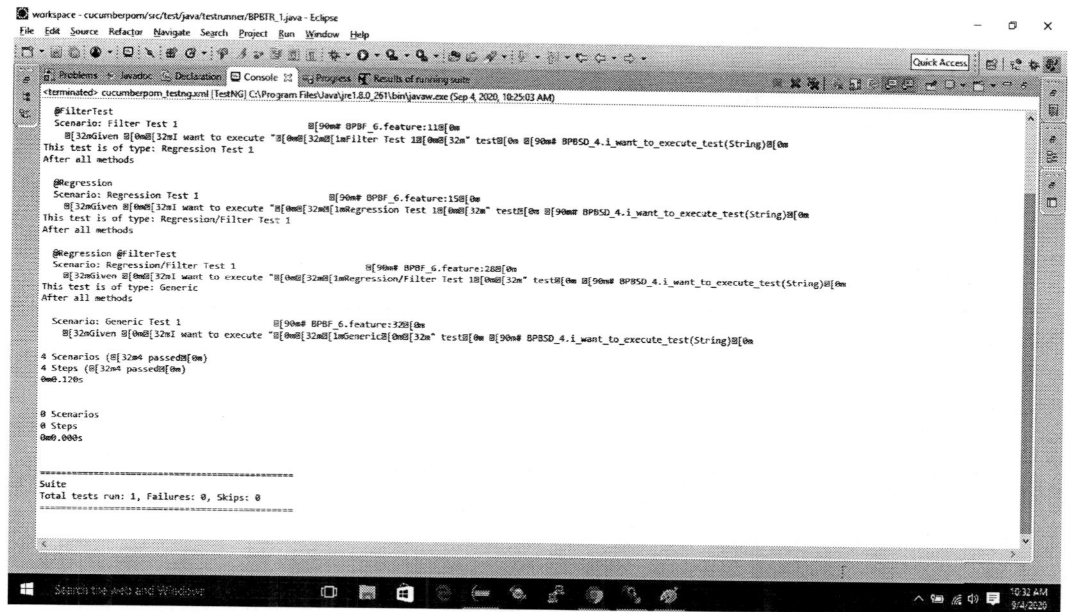

Figure 4.6: Tags with NOT condition

We covered a lot of ground in this chapter. We looked at TestNG TestRunner and the various components related to it. This concludes the chapter on Test Runners.

Conclusion

This chapter covered concepts like the Singleton Pattern and ThreadLocal. Using the Singleton Pattern and ThreadLocal concepts, we created our Singleton WebDriver class. We saw how to create a class which provides variables that can be utilized throughout the entire project. We also looked at the Test Runner and saw how to open a Chrome browser. We also learned how to open the browser of our choice. We closed the browser after each Feature file completed the execution. We learned how to create test suites with the help of tags and also learned how to provide AND, OR, and NOT conditions with these tags.

With this, we complete the components of Cucumber. This is the end of ***Part 1 - Understanding the Cucumber Framework***. The next ***Part 2 - Learning the Page Object Design Pattern*** will focus on the concepts of Page Object Design Pattern where we will first understand what a Page Object Pattern is and then we will create Page Objects for our Page Object Model framework.

Questions

1. Explain what a Singleton pattern is and its usage.
2. Explain the ThreadLocal class with example.
3. Write a Small program to create a Driver Factory using WebDriverManager library.
4. Write a small program which uses the GLOBAL_DATA class created in this chapter.
5. Write a program to create a test suite using Tags.

CHAPTER 5

The Page Object Model Without Page Factory

In *Chapter 4, Learning About the Test Runner*, we learned about the Singleton pattern, ThreadLocal class, and the WebDriver Manager library. We designed a Singleton Driver class using the WebDriverManager library and learned how to create a class with global constants. We learned about the Test Runner with TestNG specific configurations. Later, we learned how to instantiate a Chrome browser session and also learned how to open the browser of your choice. We learned how to quit the browser session. Finally, we understood what tags are and how to design a simple Test Suite with the help of tags.

We learned about the Page Object Design Pattern which is a popular pattern in test automation which reduces code duplication and simplifies code and test maintenance. The Page Object Model is derived from the Page Object Design pattern in which individual Page Objects represent the pages in AUT. Page Objects have reusable methods which interact with the web elements of the page. The Step Definitions that we created in *Chapter 3, Step Definitions* will have the code to invoke the reusable methods in the Page Objects. In the Page Object Model framework, we will have a Page Object for each Java class with locators and methods using those locators in the same class. A properties file can also be used for the locators but that involves additional code to read the property file values.

This chapter will make you an expert in designing Page Objects and help you implement the Page Object Model. By the end of this chapter, you will have classes for each page that we plan to automate.

Structure

The following topics will be covered in this chapter:

- Understanding the Page Object Design Pattern
- Understanding the Page Object Model
- Introducing the By class
- Designing a Login scenario
- Creating the Page Objects and verifying the name on Home Page
- Verifying the text on a page using the Assert class

Objectives

After reading this chapter, the reader will be able to:

- Understand the Page Object Design pattern.
- Learn about the Page Object Model.
- Design a scenario for the test.
- Create locators using the 'By' class.
- Create methods to perform operations on these Locators.
- Call these methods from the Step Definition.

5.1 Understanding the Page Object Design Pattern

The Page Object Design Pattern is a popular design pattern in test automation which is used for enhanced test maintenance and reduced code duplication. A page object is a Java class or any other OOP language class that represents a page of our AUT. The test classes which in our case will be the Step Definitions make use of the methods of this page object class whenever an action has to be performed on a page. The advantage of having such a structure is that if the UI changes for a particular page, there is no need of changing the tests. Only the Page Object classes undergo change. Hence, all changes required for the new UI are located in one place.

The Page Object Design Pattern has the following advantages:

- There is a clear separation between test code and page-specific code such as locators and the methods that operate on those locators.
- Since the locators are maintained in the **`Page Object`** class, the tests are clean with no locators scattered in them.

Now that we know what a Page Object Design pattern is, let's take a look at the Page Object Model.

5.2 What is the Page Object Model?

The Page Object Model is derived from the Page Object Design pattern. Here, we will design a class for each page. This will be a Java class in our case. Let's see the Login screen as shown in the following screenshot. We will consider this page and see a code snippet.

Click on the '**`LOG IN`**' tab to navigate to the Login Page:

Figure 5.1: The Landing Page

We create a class called **`LandingPage.java:`**

```
package pageobjects;

package pageobjects;

import org.openqa.selenium.By;

import singletondriver.SingletonDriver;

public class LandingPage extends AbstractBasePage{
       By btnLogin = By.xpath("//a[@href='https://ui.freecrm.com']");

       public void clickLogin() {
              SingletonDriver.getInstance().getDrvr().
findElement(btnLogin).click();
```

```
        }

        @Override
        public void setPageTitle(String pageTitle) {
                this.pageTitle=pageTitle;

        }

        @Override
        public String getPageTitle() {
                return this.pageTitle;
        }
}
```

In the preceding code, we have made use of the **By** class to create a locator for the Login button highlighted above. We use this locator in our method to perform the click action. Thus, everything related to this landing page will be present in the Landing page class.

In the Step Definition, we will simply create an object of the **`LandingPage`** class and invoke the **`clickLogin()`** method on it.

Since we made use of BY class above, let's dive deeper into the BY class.

5.3 Introducing the BY class

In order to locate elements, we make use of the **BY** class in Selenium. The **BY** class is an abstract class and has 8 static methods along with 8 inner classes. The 8 static methods help us locate elements based on ID, cssSelector, name, link text, class name, tag name, partial link text. and xpath. In *section 5.2,* we saw the use of xpath to locate the Login button.

We will see a code skeleton for the BY class as follows:

```
public abstract class By {
           public static By id(String id);
public static By cssSelector(String css);
public static By name(String name);
public static By linkText(String text);
           public static By className(String className);
           public static By tagName(String tagName);
```

```
        public static By partialLinkText(String partialLinkText);
        public static By xpath(String xpath);
        public static class ById extends By {
                WebElement findElement(By by);
                List <WebElement> findElements(By by);
    }
}
```

Inner classes that are present correspond to the 8 static methods. The signature of all 8 methods is shown as follows:

- **`By.id`**: Makes use of the **`id`** attribute to locate the WebElement. For example, **`By.id("dummyid").`**
- **`By.name`**: Makes use of the **`name`** attribute to locate the WebElement. For example, **`By.name("dummyname").`**
- **`By.className`**: Makes use of the **`class`** attribute to locate the WebElement. For example,**`By.className("dummyclass").`**
- **`By.linkText`**: Makes use of the text of any anchor link to locate the WebElement. For example, **`By.linkText("Click here to Login").`**
- **`By.partialLinkText`**: Makes use of the partial text of any anchor link to locate the WebElement. For example, **`By.partialLinkText("dummyText").`**
- **`By.xpath`**: Makes use of the XPath to locate the WebElement. For example, **`By.xpath("//*[text()='Login']").`**
- **`By.cssSelector`**: Makes use of the CSS selectors to locate the WebElement. For example, **`By.cssSelector(".dummy-p").`**
- **`By.tagName`**: Makes use of tag names such as **`button, select,`** and so on to locate the WebElement. For example, **`By.tagName("dummyinput").`**

Let's design a Login Scenario for our Page Object Model.

5.4 Designing a login scenario

In order to work with the automation of functional scenarios, we need to design a scenario for the Cucumber test execution. We will design a scenario in which we open a browser window, navigate to the **www.freecrm.com** website and click on the **`Login`** button. With this, we will navigate to the Login Page. We enter the username and password and click on the **`Login`** button on this page. After a successful login, we will verify the username displayed on top. The text to be verified is passed through the Feature file.

We need to perform the following steps:

1. Open the browser.
2. Navigate to the website **http://www.freecrm.com**.
3. Click on the **Login** button.
4. Enter the UserName.
5. Enter the Password.
6. Click on the **Login** button.
7. Verify the User Name on top.
8. Close the browser.

Let's take a look at our Feature file:

HappyFlowFeature.feature

```
Feature: To verify text on Homepage of www.freecrm.com

  Scenario: To verify user name on Homepage
    Given I open the "chrome" browser on "windows" and "local"
    When User navigates to the landing page
    And clicks the Login button on the landing page
    And User enters "chaubalpinakin@gmail.com" as username
    And User enters "Pc9121975!" as password
    And User clicks the Login button
    Then User should be shown "Pinakin Chaubal" on top left corner
```

***Figure 5.2**: The Login Scenario*

We have four pages to design. So let's go step by step and as the first step, let's design the Abstract Base Page Object which will serve to be a parent class for all other Page Objects.

5.5 Creating the Page Objects

In this section, we will learn how to create the three page objects starting with the parent of all Page Objects, which is the Abstract Base Page.

5.5.1 Creating the Abstract Base Page

We will create an abstract Base Page class that will serve as a base class of all Page Object classes. Right now, this page contains concrete methods for opening the browser and navigating to a URL. It also has abstract methods for setting and getting the Page Title. The Abstract Base Page class will have the openBrowser(String, String, String) and **navigateURL()** methods which are the two concrete methods. The URL is picked up from the **GLOBAL_DATA** class. The entry in the **GLOBAL_DATA** class is shown as follows:

```
public static final String URL="http://freecrm.co.in";
```

The **AbstractBasePage** class is shown as follows:

```
package pageobjects;

import constants.GLOBAL_DATA;
import singletondriver.SingletonDriver;

public abstract class AbstractBasePage {
	protected String pageTitle;
	public void navigateURL() {
		SingletonDriver.getInstance().getDrvr().navigate().
to(GLOBAL_DATA.URL);
	}

	public void openBrowser(String browserName, String platform, 
String gridSetting) {
		try {
			SingletonDriver.getInstance().setDrvr(browserName, 
platform, gridSetting, null);
		} catch (Exception e) {
			// TODO Auto-generated catch block
			e.printStackTrace();
		}

	}

	public abstract void setPageTitle(String pageTitle);
	public abstract String getPageTitle();

}
```

Next, we will make use of inheritance and create three Page Objects, namely, LandingPage, LoginPage, and Homepage which extend this abstract class. Since our Page objects are concrete classes, we have to provide a method body for the two methods **setPageTitle(String pageTitle)** and **getPageTitle()**. Since we have the SingletonDriver already set up, we make use of it to create an instance of the Chrome Driver and navigate to the **http://freecrm.co**.in website. The **navigateURL** method lands us on the Landing page so that we can use it to click on the **Login** button that is in the Landing page.

Let's design the Landing page next.

5.5.2 Creating the Landing Page

The Landing page is the one that loads when the browser is opened and navigation happens to **http://freecrm.co.in**. Our only task on this page is to click on the **Login** button and land us on the Login Page. Let's see how we can implement the Landing Page.

The Landing page extends the Abstract Base Page as follows:

```
package pageobjects;

import org.openqa.selenium.By;

import singletondriver.SingletonDriver;

public class LandingPage extends AbstractBasePage{
	By btnLogin = By.xpath("//a[@href='https://ui.freecrm.com']");

	public void clickLogin() {
		SingletonDriver.getInstance().getDrvr().
findElement(btnLogin).click();
	}

	@Override
	public void setPageTitle(String pageTitle) {
		this.pageTitle=pageTitle;


	}


	@Override
	public String getPageTitle() {
		return this.pageTitle;
	}
}
```

We created a **By** locator for the Login button using xpath. We have a **`clickLogin()`** method that clicks the Login button and lands us on the LoginPage so that it can be used further. We have also implemented the abstracts methods from the Abstract Base Page, namely, **`setPageTitle(String)`** and **`getPageTitle()`**.

Now that we are on the **`LoginPage`**, let's see how we can implement the **`LoginPage`** class.

5.5.3 Creating the login page

The **`LoginPage`** class has three WebElements to work with, namely, UserName textbox, Password textbox, and Login button. By clicking on the **`Login`** button, the user can navigate to the HomePage so that we can extract and verify the User Name displayed on top.

The Login page also extends the Abstract Base Page as follows:

```
package pageobjects;

import org.openqa.selenium.By;

import singletondriver.SingletonDriver;

public class LoginPage extends AbstractBasePage{
	By email = By.name("email");
	By password = By.name("password");
	By btnLogin = By.xpath("//div[text()='Login']");
	public void enterUserName(String userName) {
		SingletonDriver.getInstance().getDrvr().findElement(email).
sendKeys(userName);
	}
	public void enterPassword(String passwordtxt) {
		SingletonDriver.getInstance().getDrvr().
findElement(password).sendKeys(passwordtxt);
	}
	public void clickLogin() {
		SingletonDriver.getInstance().getDrvr().
findElement(btnLogin).click();
	}
	@Override
```

```
        public void setPageTitle(String pageTitle) {
                this.pageTitle = pageTitle;

        }
        @Override
        public String getPageTitle() {
                return this.pageTitle;
        }
}
```

Now we are on the HomePage and we are in the final phase of verification of the UserName on the top panel. Let's see the **Homepage.java** next.

5.5.4 Creating the Home Page

Now that we are on the Homepage, we make use of the **getText()** method to capture the text present for the UserName on the top panel. The procedure remains the same. We will create a variable of type 'By' for the UserName span. We also have the Logout functionality scripted in this class since the Logout appears on the HomePage after Logging In. Logout is a two-step process where the Logout icon is clicked first followed by clicking of the '**Log out**' link. We can quit the browser after this. All this code has been kept in the **logOut()** method which is annotated with **@After** which ensures that this is run after every Feature.

The Homepage page object verifies the Username on the top of the page which is shown as follows:

```
package pageobjects;

import org.openqa.selenium.By;
import org.testng.Assert;

import cucumber.api.java.After;
import singletondriver.SingletonDriver;

public class Homepage extends AbstractBasePage{

        By userDisplay = By.xpath("//span[@class='user-display']");
        By logOutDiv = By.xpath("//div[@role='listbox']");
        By logOutSpan = By.xpath("//span[text()='Log Out']");
```

```
	public void verifyUser(String userDisplayText) {
		System.out.println(SingletonDriver.getInstance().getDrvr().
findElement(userDisplay).getText());
		Assert.assertEquals(SingletonDriver.getInstance().
getDrvr().findElement(userDisplay).getText(), userDisplayText);
	}

	@After
	public void logOut() {
		SingletonDriver.getInstance().getDrvr().
findElement(logOutDiv).click();
		SingletonDriver.getInstance().getDrvr().
findElement(logOutSpan).click();
		SingletonDriver.getInstance().getDrvr().close();
		SingletonDriver.getInstance().getDrvr().quit();
	}

	@Override
	public void setPageTitle(String title) {
		this.pageTitle=pageTitle;

	}

	@Override
	public String getPageTitle() {
		return this.pageTitle;
	}
}
```

Let's understand the Step Definitions next.

5.6 Step definitions for the pages

In *section 5.5,* we designed the three-page objects along with the Abstract Base Page. We have segregated our Step Definitions in three separate Java classes. Let's see each Java class.

5.6.1 Landing Page Step definition

Let's take a look at the Landing page step definitions. The first thing we do in this Step Definition is to create an object of the LandingPage. Using this object, we open a Chrome browser, navigate to the URL, and click on the **Login** button. Notice that the methods for opening a browser and navigating to the URL are present in the AbstractBasePage and not in the landing page, but since we have extended the Abstract Base Page for all our page objects, we can use the LandingPage object to invoke methods in the Abstract Base Page.

The LandingStepDef Step Definition that makes use of the **LandingPage** page object is shown as follows:

```
package stepdefinitions;

import constants.GLOBAL_DATA;
import cucumber.api.java.en.Given;
import cucumber.api.java.en.When;
import pageobjects.LandingPage;

public class LandingStepDef {

	LandingPage = new LandingPage();

	@Given("^I open the \"([^\"]*)\" browser on \"([^\"]*)\" and 
\"([^\"]*)\"$")
	public void i_open_the_browser_on_and(String browser, String 
platform, String gridSetting) throws Throwable {
		landingPage.openBrowser(browser, platform, gridSetting);
	}

	@When("^User navigates to the landing page$")
	public void user_navigates_to_the_landing_page() throws Throwable 
{
		landingPage.navigateURL();
	}

	@When("^clicks the Login button on the landing page$")
	public void clicks_the_Login_button_on_the_landing_page() throws 
Throwable {
		landingPage.clickLogin();
	}

}
```

Now that we have navigated to the Login Page, let's move on to the Login Page Step Definition.

5.6.2 Login Page Step Definition

Next in our list is the design of the Login Page Step Definition. Here, our task is to enter the email, password, and then click on the **Login** button. The code for the Login Page Step Definition is shown below. It basically has the same structure as the Landing Page Step Definition. We create an object of the LoginPage and then we enter the UserName, Password, and then click on the Login button using this object.

LoginStepDef makes use of the LoginPage page object as follows:

```
package stepdefinitions;

import cucumber.api.java.en.And;
import cucumber.api.java.en.When;
import pageobjects.LoginPage;

public class LoginStepDef {

        LoginPage = new LoginPage();
        @When("^User enters \"(.*?)\" as username$")
        public void user_enters_admin_as_username(String userName) throws
Throwable {
                System.out.println("UserName is: "+userName);
                loginPage.enterUserName(userName);
        }

        @And("^User enters \"(.*?)\" as password$")
        public void user_enters_admin_as_password(String password) throws
Throwable {
                System.out.println("Password is: "+password);
                loginPage.enterPassword(password);
        }

        @And("^User clicks the Login button$")
        public void user_clicks_the_Login_button() throws Throwable {
                System.out.println("Login button clicked");
                loginPage.clickLogin();
```

```
        }

}
```

Finally, we move to the Homepage step definition.

5.6.3 Home Page step definition

The Home Page step definition has a similar code structure to the landing page step definition and login page step definition. The code listing is given as follows:

```
package stepdefinitions;

import cucumber.api.java.en.Then;
import pageobjects.Homepage;

public class HomePageStepDef {
        Homepage = new Homepage();
        @Then("^User should be shown \"(.*?)\" on top left corner$")
        public void user_should_be_shown_User_Name_on_top_left_
corner(String userDisplayText) throws Throwable {
                System.out.println("UserName verified");
                homePage.verifyUser(userDisplayText);
        }

}
```

This is a comparatively small code listing, wherein we just validate the text displayed on top of the page with that passed from the Feature file. We have used the Assert class to accomplish this and the Assert class verification is what we will see next.

5.7 Verification of text on a page using the Assert class

In the code listing of *section 5.6*, we have invoked the **`verifyUser(String)`** method from the Homepage Page Object. This Page Object had made use of the **`assertEquals`** method from the **`Assert`** class. This method is provided the following arguments: an actual string and an expected string. The actual string is the text extracted from the WebElement named **`userDisplay`** and this string is extracted using the following code snippet:

```
        SingletonDriver.getInstance().getDrvr().findElement(userDisplay).
getText()
```

The Expected string value is taken from the Feature file. The line from the Feature file shown as follows provides this value.

Then, the User should be shown "*Pinakin Chaubal*" on top-left hand corner of the page.

If we change the string in the preceding line to "Pinakin Chaubal1", the test now fails with an Assertion error shown as follows:

```
<terminated> HappyFlowFeature.feature [Cucumber Feature] C:\Program Files\Java\jre1.8.0_261\bin\javaw.exe (Sep 7, 2020, 2:43:14 PM)
  Scenario: To verify user name on Homepage                           # D:/pinakin.chaubal/workspace/cucumberpom/src/test/resources/featurefiles/HappyFlowFeature.feature:3
    Given I open the "chrome" browser on "windows" and "local"        # LandingStepDef.i_open_the_browser_on_and(String,String,String)
    When User navigates to the landing page                           # LandingStepDef.user_navigates_to_the_landing_page()
    And clicks the Login button on the landing page                   # LandingStepDef.clicks_the_Login_button_on_the_landing_page()
    And User enters "chaubalpinakin@gmail.com" as username            # LoginStepDef.user_enters_admin_as_username(String)
    And User enters "Pc9121975!" as password                          # LoginStepDef.user_enters_admin_as_password(String)
    And User clicks the Login button                                  # LoginStepDef.user_clicks_the_Login_button()
    Then User should be shown "Pinakin Chaubal1" on top left corner # HomePageStepDef.user_should_be_shown_User_Name_on_top_left_corner(String)
      java.lang.AssertionError: expected [Pinakin Chaubal1] but found [Pinakin Chaubal]
        at org.testng.Assert.fail(Assert.java:96)
        at org.testng.Assert.failNotEquals(Assert.java:776)
        at org.testng.Assert.assertEqualsImpl(Assert.java:137)
        at org.testng.Assert.assertEquals(Assert.java:118)
        at org.testng.Assert.assertEquals(Assert.java:453)
        at org.testng.Assert.assertEquals(Assert.java:463)
        at pageobjects.Homepage.verifyUser(Homepage.java:17)
        at stepdefinitions.HomePageStepDef.user_should_be_shown_User_Name_on_top_left_corner(HomePageStepDef.java:11)
        at ?.Then User should be shown "Pinakin Chaubal1" on top left corner(D:/pinakin.chaubal/workspace/cucumberpom/src/test/resources/featurefiles/HappyFlowFeature.feature:10)

Failed scenarios:
D:/pinakin.chaubal/workspace/cucumberpom/src/test/resources/featurefiles/HappyFlowFeature.feature:3 # Scenario: To verify user name on Homepage

1 Scenarios (1 failed)
7 Steps (1 failed, 6 passed)
0m29.910s

java.lang.AssertionError: expected [Pinakin Chaubal1] but found [Pinakin Chaubal]
        at org.testng.Assert.fail(Assert.java:96)
        at org.testng.Assert.failNotEquals(Assert.java:776)
        at org.testng.Assert.assertEqualsImpl(Assert.java:137)
        at org.testng.Assert.assertEquals(Assert.java:118)
        at org.testng.Assert.assertEquals(Assert.java:453)
        at org.testng.Assert.assertEquals(Assert.java:463)
        at pageobjects.Homepage.verifyUser(Homepage.java:17)
        at stepdefinitions.HomePageStepDef.user_should_be_shown_User_Name_on_top_left_corner(HomePageStepDef.java:11)
        at ?.Then User should be shown "Pinakin Chaubal1" on top left corner(D:/pinakin.chaubal/workspace/cucumberpom/src/test/resources/featurefiles/HappyFlowFeature.feature:10)
```

Figure 5.3*: Assertion failure of Username verification*

With this, we come to the end of this chapter. We covered all concepts related to the Page Object Model without Page Factory.

Conclusion

This chapter covered the concept of the Page Object Model without PageFactory using Java. We started by understanding what the Page Object Design Pattern is. We learned about the Page Object Model. We learned the **`BY`** class which is at the heart of the Page Object Model and took a brief look at the methods associated with the **`BY`** class. We next designed our Login Scenario by creating a Feature file. We created the Abstract Base Page class along with the three Page Objects for the Landing Page, Login Page, and Home Page. Finally, we saw how to verify the text present on the Homepage using the **`assertEquals`** method of the **`Assert`** class.

In the next chapter, we will take a look at how to create the Page Objects Model with PageFactory. We will take a look at the **`@FindBy`** annotation which can be used to create a locator. We will also take a look at what **`@CacheLookup`** is and how it can speed up test execution with the help of WebElement caching. We will create a class of Locators and keep it separate from the corresponding Page Object.

Questions

1. Explain what a Page Object Model is without PageFactory.
2. Explain the components of the 'BY' class.
3. Write a small program to take a sample web page and create a Page Object for it.
4. Create a Page Object Model for logging into **www.gmail.com** and verifying the UserName.
5. Explain the different methods of the Assert class.

CHAPTER 6

Learning About the Page Object Model Using Page Factory

In *Chapter 5, Page Object Model without Page Factory*, we learned how to design Page Objects and used them in the Page Object Model framework without Page Factory. We learned the theory behind the Page Object Design pattern and then understood the Page Object Model. We learned about the BY class and its usage in the design of Page Objects. We designed a simple Login Scenario in the form of a Feature file. We created an Abstract Base Page which was inherited by the Landing Page, Login Page, and Home Page. Finally, we verified the username on the Home Page.

In this chapter, we will learn about the Page Object Model using PageFactory which is a popular pattern in test automation which reduces code duplication and simplifies code and test maintenance. PageFactory makes use of the `@FindBy` annotation which we will learn in this chapter. Each AUT page will have two Java classes attached to it, namely, the Page Object class itself and the Page Object Locators class which will be used by the Page Object class. A concept known as Composition in Java will be covered in this respect. We will create a different set of Java classes and a Feature file for this chapter.

This chapter will make you an expert in designing Page Objects and implementing the Page Object Model using PageFactory. By the end of this chapter, you will have two classes for each page that we plan to automate.

The following topics will be covered in this chapter:

- Understanding the Page Factory Design pattern
- Learning about the **`PageFactory`** class
- Introducing the **`@FindBy`**, **`@FindBys,`** and **`@FindAll`** annotations
- Understanding the **`initElements`** method
- Designing the Page Factory framework
- Designing a Login Scenario
- Creating the Page Locators using **`@FindBy`**
- Creating the Page Objects
- Using composition to include the locator in the Page Objects
- Creating the Step Definitions
- Understanding the **`@CacheLookup`** annotation

Objectives

After reading this chapter, the reader will be able to:

- Understand the Page Factory Design pattern.
- Learn about the **`PageFactory`** class.
- Understand the **`@FindBy`**, **`@FindBys,`** and **`@FindAll`** annotations.
- Understand the **`initElements`** method.
- Design our Page Factory framework.
- Design a scenario for the test.
- Create a class for locators using the '**`@FindBy`**' annotation.
- Create methods to perform operations on these Locators.
- Call these methods from the Step Definition.
- Get familiar with the **`@CacheLookup`** annotation.

6.1 Understanding the Page Factory Design pattern

The Page Factory Design pattern is an extension to the Page Object Design pattern but is much more advanced. The creation of Page Objects is simplified by using the Page Factory pattern. The elements in the Page Objects can be initialized using the static method of the **`PageFactory`** class which is **`initElements()`**. The **`PageFactory.`**

initElements() static method takes two arguments, namely, the driver instance and the class type, and it returns a Page Object with its variables/fields which are initialized. The locators and the code using those locators can be in the same or different class. Generally, a different class is preferable.

The Page Factory Design pattern has the following advantages:

- The WebElements of a web page are initialized at one go.
- Since the locators are maintained in the Page Object class, the tests are clean with no locators scattered in them.

Now that we know what a Page Factory Design pattern is, let's take a look at the **PageFactory** class.

6.2 Learning about the PageFactory class

The WebDriver library provides us with the **PageFactory** class so that we can create our Page Objects with ease. This ease of creating Page Objects is due to the annotations provided by the **PageFactory** class. WebElements can be pre-defined in the class and the PageFactory transforms the WebElements into Proxied objects where the Java proxy class is utilized. When the time comes to make use of these WebElements, the annotations provided by the PageFactory class transform the proxy objects in WebElements so that the WebElements can be used. A two-step process needs to be used:

- Annotate the variables that we need to use (proxy) in our code.
- Initialize the proxied elements with the **initElements()** method before using them.

Let's first understand how to annotate the variables that we need to proxy.

6.3 Introducing the @FindBy, @FindBys, and @FindAll annotations

Let us see the various annotations that Cucumber provides. We will look at three annotations, namely, **@FindBy**, **@FindBys,** and **@FindAll**. Let's start with the **@ FindBy** annotation.

6.3.1 The @FindBy annotation

@FindBy is an annotation which specifies the Object Location strategy for a single WebElement or list of WebElements. The **@FindBy** annotation is used to find one or more WebElements using single search criteria. If we are sure that our search criteria will return a single WebElement, then we can use the annotation as follows:

```
@FindBy(how=How.XPATH,using="//a[@href='https://ui.freecrm.com']")
public  WebElement btnLogin;
```

Here, the location strategy is specified using the XPATH strategy from the **HOW** enum. Here, we will find the WebElement with XPath `//a[@href='https://ui.freecrm.com']` and assign it to the WebElement **`btnLogin`**.

If we are not sure about the number of WebElements returned by the search criteria, use a **`List<WebElement>`** instead of a single WebElement as follows:

```
@FindBy(how=How.CLASS_NAME,using="dummyclass")
public  List<WebElement> txtBoxes;
```

Here, the location strategy is specified using the CLASS_NAME strategy from the **HOW** enum. Here, we will find the WebElement with Class Name `dummyclass` and assign it to a list of WebElements **txtBoxes.** We then need additional code to iterate through this list of WebElements.

Let's next take a look at the **`@FindBys`** annotation.

6.3.2 The @FindBys annotation

When we need to find WebElements that match all of the given criteria, then in such a case **`@FindBys`** is used. More than single search criteria can be specified as follows:

```
@FindBys({
        @FindBy(how = How.ID, using = "dummyid"),
        @FindBy(how = How.NAME, using = "dummyname")
})
private List<WebElement> bothMatching;
```

In the preceding example, the list of WebElements will include WebElements which have the ID as '**`dummyid`**' and NAME as '**`dummyname`**'.

Let's see the **`@FindAll`** annotation next.

6.3.3 The @FindAll annotation

When we need to find WebElements that match at least one of the given criteria, then in such a case, **`@FindAll`** is used. More than single search criteria can be specified as follows:

```
@FindAll({
        @FindBy(how = How.ID, using = "dummyid"),
```

```
        @FindBy(how = How.NAME, using = "dummyname")
})
private List<WebElement> atleastOneMatching;
```

In the preceding example, the list of WebElements will include WebElements which have the ID as '**dummyid**' or NAME as '**dummyname**'.

Let's see how to initialize the proxied elements with the **initElements()** method before using them in the code.

6.4 Understanding the initElements method

In this section, we will take a look at step two of *section 6.2* which is about initializing the proxied elements. The **PageFactory** class provides us with a static **initElements** method which can be used for this purpose. There are three overloaded versions of this method which are as follows:

- `public static void initElements(WebDriver driver, java.lang.Object page)`

  This is the basic version which takes a WebDriver and page class as arguments.

- `public static void initElements(ElementLocatorFactory factory, java.lang.Object page)`

  This version takes a **ElementLocatorFactory** that is used to provide a mechanism for finding elements and page class as arguments.

- `public static void initElements(FieldDecorator field, java.lang.Object page)`

  This version takes a FieldDecorator that is used to decorate each of the fields.

We will see the annotations and the **initElements()** method in action when we explore the sample scenario.

6.5 Designing the Page Factory framework

We will use a similar structure as the Page Object Model. We will create two additional packages under **src/main/java,** namely, **pageobjectspf**, where the 'pf' at the end stands for Page Factory and locators, which will have Java classes with the **@FindBy** annotation. Public WebElements will be maintained in these classes so that they are accessible for the Java classes that utilize these variables. All Page Objects will inherit an **AbstractBasePagePF** class. This class will have two concrete methods,

openBrowser(String, String, String) and **navigateURL()**. It will also have two abstract methods for getting and setting the Page Title. Since we have three pages to work with, we will have three page objects and three step definitions.

The Page Factory framework designed in such a manner will help splitting the work of creating the Object Repository [Classes for Locators] and Page Objects and can be done independently of each other without dependencies involved.

6.6 Designing a Login scenario

We will start with a simple scenario as follows:

1. Open the browser.
2. Navigate to the website **http://www.freecrm.com.**
3. Click on the **Login** button.
4. Enter UserName.
5. Enter Password.
6. Click on the **Login** button.
7. Verify the User Name on top of page.
8. Close the browser.

Let's take a look at our Feature file as shown in the following screenshot:

*HappyFlowFeaturePF.feature

```
Feature: To verify text on Homepage of www.freecrm.com

  Scenario: To verify user name on Homepage
    Given The user opens the "chrome" browser on "windows" and "local"
    When The user navigates to the landing page
    And The user clicks the Login button on the landing page
    And The user enters "chaubalpinakin@gmail.com" as username
    And The user enters "Pc9121975!" as password
    And The user clicks the Login button
    Then The user should be shown "Pinakin Chaubal" on top left corner
```

***Figure 6.1**: Login Scenario*

We have three pages for the locators to design. So let's go step by step and as the first step, let's design the locators for the Landing Page, Login Page, and Home Page which will be used by their respective Page Objects.

6.7 Creating the Page Locators using @ FindBy

In this section, we will create the locator classes for the Landing Page, Login Page, and Home Page. This class will have locators designed as per the Page Factory style with the **@FindBy** annotation.

Let's start with the locators for the Landing Page.

6.7.1 Creating the Landing Page Locators

The landing page has the Login button that needs to be clicked to open the Login page. Here is the content of the **LandingPageLocators.java** that has one WebElement defined with the **@FindBy** annotation:

```
package locators;

import org.openqa.selenium.WebElement;
import org.openqa.selenium.support.FindBy;
import org.openqa.selenium.support.How;

public class LandingPageLocators {

	@FindBy(how=How.XPATH,using="//a[@href='https://ui.freecrm.
com']")
	public  WebElement btnLogin;

}
```

This is a straightforward class with just one WebElement for the **Login** button. We are locating the Login button using the XPath strategy.

6.7.2 Creating the Login Page locators

The login page has the email address and password text boxes and the **Login** button. Here is the content of the **LoginPageLocators.java** that has three WebElements defined with the **@FindBy** annotation:

```
package locators;

import org.openqa.selenium.WebElement;
import org.openqa.selenium.support.FindBy;
import org.openqa.selenium.support.How;
```

```
public class LoginPageLocators {

        @FindBy(name="email")
        public WebElement email;

@FindBy(name="password")
        public WebElement password;

@FindBy(how=How.XPATH,using="//div[text()='Login']")
        public WebElement btnLogin;

}
```

This class finds elements based on the name as well as the X-Path Strategy.

6.7.3 Creating the Home Page locators

The Home page has the User Name display on top that needs to be verified. In addition to this, it also has the LogOut Div and LogOut span. Here is the content of the **HomePageLocators.java** that has three WebElements defined with the **@ FindBy** annotation:

```
package locators;

import org.openqa.selenium.WebElement;
import org.openqa.selenium.support.FindBy;
import org.openqa.selenium.support.How;

public class HomepageLocators {

        @FindBy(how=How.XPATH,using="//span[@class='user-display']")
        public WebElement userDisplay;

        @FindBy(how=How.XPATH,using="//div[@role='listbox']")
        public WebElement logOutDiv;

        @FindBy(how=How.XPATH,using="//span[text()='Log Out']")
        public WebElement logOutSpan;

}
```

This class finds elements based on the X-Path Strategy. Now that we have created individual classes for the locators, let's go ahead and design our Page Objects. There are four classes involved: The Abstract Base Page, Landing Page Object, Login Page Object, and Home Page object.

6.8 Creating the Page Objects

In this section, we will learn how to create the three page objects starting with the parent of all Page Objects, which is the Abstract Base Page.

6.8.1 Creating the Abstract Base Page

We will create an abstract Base Page class that will serve as a base class of all Page Object classes. Right now, this page contains concrete methods for opening the browser and navigating to a URL. It also has abstract methods for setting and getting the Page Title. The Abstract Base Page class will have the **openBrowser(String, String, String)** and **navigateURL()** methods which are the two concrete methods. The URL is picked up from the **GLOBAL_DATA** class. The entry in the **GLOBAL_DATA** class is as follows:

```
public static final String URL="http://freecrm.co.in";
```

The **AbstractBasePage** class is shown as follows:

```
package pageobjectspf;

import constants.GLOBAL_DATA;
import pageobjectspf.LandingPagePF;
import singletondriver.SingletonDriver;

public abstract class AbstractBasePagePF {
	protected String pageTitle;

	public LandingPagePF navigateURL() {
		SingletonDriver.getInstance().getDrvr().navigate().
to(GLOBAL_DATA.URL);
		return new LandingPagePF();
	}

	public void openBrowser(String browserName, String platform,
String gridSetting) {
		try {
```

```
                    SingletonDriver.getInstance().setDrvr(browserName,
platform, gridSetting, null);
            } catch (Exception e) {
                    // TODO Auto-generated catch block
                    e.printStackTrace();
            }

    }

    public abstract void setPageTitle(String pageTitle);
    public abstract String getPageTitle();

}
```

Note that the **navigateURL** returns an object of the **LandingPage** when the control is sent back to the child class **LandingPage** that inherits the **AbstractBasePagePF** class. When we see the Step Definitions in the later section, we will see how to get a hold of this returned object to do actions on the Landing Page.

Next, we will make use of inheritance and create three Page Objects, namely, LandingPage, LoginPage, and Homepage which extend this abstract class. Since our Page objects are concrete classes, we have to provide a method body for the two methods **setPageTitle(String pageTitle)** and **getPageTitle()**. Since we have the SingletonDriver already set up, we make use of it to create an instance of the Chrome Driver and navigate to the **http://freecrm.co.in** website. The **navigateURL** method lands us on the Landing page so that we can use it to click on the **Login** button that is in the Landing page.

Let's design the Landing page next.

6.8.2 Creating the Landing Page

The Landing page is the one which loads when the browser is opened and navigation happens in **http://freecrm.co.in**. Our only task on this page is to click on the **Login** button and land on the Login Page. Let's see how we have implemented the Landing Page. The Landing page extends the Abstract Base Page. We will use the concept of composition and create an object of the **LandingPageLocators** class inside the **LandingPagePF** page object. Inside the constructor, we will instantiate the **landingPageLocators** object and initialize all WebElements at one go using the **initElements** method which takes as argument the driver instance and the **LandingPageLocators** object.

```
package pageobjectspf;
```

```
import org.openqa.selenium.support.PageFactory;

import locators.LandingPageLocators;
import singletondriver.SingletonDriver;

public class LandingPagePF extends AbstractBasePagePF{

	LandingPageLocators;

	public LandingPagePF() {
		super();
		landingpageLocators = new LandingPageLocators();
		PageFactory.initElements(SingletonDriver.getInstance().
getDrvr(), landingpageLocators);
		System.out.println("After init");
	}

	public void clickLogin() {
		System.out.println("Before click"+this.landingpageLocators.
btnLogin.getText());
		landingpageLocators.btnLogin.click();
		System.out.println("After click");
	}

	@Override
	public void setPageTitle(String pageTitle) {
		this.pageTitle=pageTitle;

	}

	@Override
	public String getPageTitle() {
		return this.pageTitle;
	}
}
```

We have a **`clickLogin()`** method that clicks the **`Login`** button and lands us on LoginPage so that it can be used further. We have also implemented the abstracts methods from the Abstract Base Page, namely, **`setPageTitle(String)`** and **`getPageTitle()`**.

Now that we are on the LoginPage, let's see how we can implement the **LoginPage** class.

6.8.3 Creating the Login page

The **LoginPage** class has three WebElements to work with, namely, **UserName** textbox, **Password** textbox, and **Login** button. After clicking on the **Login** button, the user needs to navigate to the HomePage so that we can extract and verify the User Name displayed on the top:

```
package pageobjectspf;

import org.openqa.selenium.support.PageFactory;

import locators.LoginPageLocators;
import singletondriver.SingletonDriver;

public class LoginPagePF extends AbstractBasePagePF{
	LoginPageLocators;

	public LoginPagePF() {
		super();
		loginpageLocators = new LoginPageLocators();
		PageFactory.initElements(SingletonDriver.getInstance().
getDrvr(), loginpageLocators);
	}

	public void enterUserName(String userName) {
		loginpageLocators.email.sendKeys(userName);
	}
	public void enterPassword(String passwordtxt) {
		loginpageLocators.password.sendKeys(passwordtxt);
	}
	public void clickLogin() {
		loginpageLocators.btnLogin.click();
	}
	@Override
	public void setPageTitle(String pageTitle) {
		this.pageTitle = pageTitle;
```

```
        }
        @Override
        public String getPageTitle() {
                return this.pageTitle;
        }
}
```

Now we are on the HomePage and we are in the final phase of verification of the UserName on the top panel. Let's see the **`Homepage.java`** next.

6.8.4 Creating the Home page

Now that we are on the Homepage, we will make use of the **`getText()`** method to capture the text present for UserName on the top panel. The procedure remains the same. We have the Logout functionality scripted in this class since the Logout appears on the HomePage after logging in. Logout is a two-step process where the Logout icon is clicked first followed by clicking on the 'Log out' link. We will quit the browser after this. All this code has been kept in the **`logOut()`** method. Logout happens after each Feature finishes execution as the **`logOut()`** method is annotated with the **`@After`** annotation.

Note: We can also keep the method annotated with the @After annotation in a different class based on requirements.

The code listing is given as follows:

```
package pageobjectspf;

import org.openqa.selenium.support.PageFactory;
import org.testng.Assert;

import locators.HomepageLocators;
import singletondriver.SingletonDriver;

public class HomepagePF extends AbstractBasePagePF{

        HomepageLocators;

        public HomepagePF() {
                super();
                homepageLocators = new HomepageLocators();
```

```
            PageFactory.initElements(SingletonDriver.getInstance().
getDrvr(), homepageLocators);
        }

        public void verifyUser(String userDisplayText) {
                System.out.println(homepageLocators.userDisplay.getText());
                Assert.assertEquals(homepageLocators.userDisplay.getText(),
userDisplayText);
        }

        @After
        public void logOut() {
                homepageLocators.logOutDiv.click();
                homepageLocators.logOutSpan.click();
                SingletonDriver.getInstance().getDrvr().close();
                SingletonDriver.getInstance().getDrvr().quit();
        }

        @Override
        public void setPageTitle(String title) {
                this.pageTitle=pageTitle;

        }

        @Override
        public String getPageTitle() {
                return this.pageTitle;
        }
}
```

With this, we are done with creating the Abstract Base page along with the three page objects for the Landing Page, Login Page, and Home Page.

Let's understand the Step definitions next.

6.9 Step definitions for the pages

In section 6.8, we designed the three page objects along with the Abstract Base Page. We have segregated our Step Definitions in three separate java classes. Let's see each Java class.

6.9.1 Landing page step definition

Let's take a look at the Landing page step definitions. The first thing we do in this Step Definition is to create an object of the LandingPage. Using this object, we will open a Chrome browser, navigate to the URL, and click on the **Login** button. Notice that the methods for opening a browser and navigating to the URL are present in the AbstractBasePage and not in the landing page but since we have extended the Abstract Base Page for all our page objects, we can use the **LandingPage** object to invoke methods in the Abstract Base Page. Also, note that we are capturing the returned **LandingPage** object from the **navigateURL()** method and making use of it to do the click operation of the **Login** button on the Landing page. The code is as follows:

```
package stepdefinitions;

import constants.GLOBAL_DATA;
import cucumber.api.java.en.Given;
import cucumber.api.java.en.When;
import pageobjects.LandingPage;
import pageobjectspf.LandingPagePF;

public class LandingStepDefPF {

	LandingPagePF landingPagePF = new LandingPagePF();

	@Given("^The user opens the \"([^\"]*)\" browser on \"([^\"]*)\" 
and \"([^\"]*)\"$")
	public void i_open_the_browser_on_and(String browser, String 
platform, String gridSetting) throws Throwable {
		landingPagePF.openBrowser(browser, platform, gridSetting);
	}

	@When("^The user navigates to the landing page$")
	public void user_navigates_to_the_landing_page() throws Throwable 
{
		landingPagePF = landingPagePF.navigateURL();
	}

	@When("^The user clicks the Login button on the landing page$")
	public void The_user_clicks_the_Login_button_on_the_landing_
page() throws Throwable {
```

```
            landingPagePF.clickLogin();
      }

}
```

Now that we have navigated to the Login page, let's move on to the Login Page Step Definition.

6.9.2 Login page step definition

Next in our list is the design of the Login Page Step Definition. Here, our task is to enter the email, password, and then click on the **Login** button. The code for the Login Page Step Definition is shown as follows. It basically has the same structure as the Landing Page Step Definition. We created an object of the **LoginPage** and then we entered the **UserName**, **Password,** and then clicked on the **Login** button using this object. The code is as follows:

```
package stepdefinitions;

import cucumber.api.java.en.And;
import cucumber.api.java.en.When;
import pageobjects.LoginPage;
import pageobjectspf.LoginPagePF;

public class LoginStepDefPF {

      LoginPagePF loginPagePF = new LoginPagePF();
      @When("^The user enters \"(.*?)\" as username$")
      public void user_enters_admin_as_username(String userName) throws
Throwable {
            System.out.println("UserName is: "+userName);
            loginPagePF.enterUserName(userName);
      }

      @And("^The user enters \"(.*?)\" as password$")
      public void user_enters_admin_as_password(String password) throws
Throwable {
            System.out.println("Password is: "+password);
            loginPagePF.enterPassword(password);
      }
```

```
        @And("^The user clicks the Login button$")
        public void user_clicks_the_Login_button() throws Throwable {
                System.out.println("Login button clicked");
                loginPagePF.clickLogin();
        }

}
```

Finally, we move on to the Homepage Step Definition.

6.9.3 Home page step definition

The Home Page step definition has a similar code structure to the Landing Page Step Definition and Login Page Step Definition. We created an object of the **HomePage** and used it to fetch the text of the **UserName**. The code listing is given as follows:

```
package stepdefinitions;

import cucumber.api.java.en.Then;
import pageobjects.Homepage;
import pageobjectspf.HomepagePF;

public class HomePageStepDefPF {
        HomepagePF homePagePF = new HomepagePF();
        @Then("^The user should be shown \"(.*?)\" on top left corner$")
        public void user_should_be_shown_User_Name_on_top_left_
corner(String userDisplayText) throws Throwable {
                System.out.println("UserName verified");
                homePagePF.verifyUser(userDisplayText);
        }

}
```

This is a comparatively small code listing, wherein we will just validate the text displayed on top of the page with that passed from the Feature file.

Once the HomePage Step Definition is completed, simply execute the Feature file '**HappyFlowFeaturePF.feature**' by doing a right click on the Feature file and selecting '**Run As->Cucumber Feature**'.

The output is as follows:

```
SLF4J: Defaulting to no-operation (NOP) logger implementation
SLF4J: See http://www.slf4j.org/codes.html#StaticLoggerBinder for further details.
log4j:WARN No appenders could be found for logger (org.apache.http.client.protocol.RequestAddCookies).
log4j:WARN Please initialize the log4j system properly.
log4j:WARN See http://logging.apache.org/log4j/1.2/faq.html#noconfig for more info.
Starting ChromeDriver 83.0.4103.39 (ccbf011cb2d2b19b506d844400483861342c20cd-refs/branch-heads/4103@{#416}) on port 27128
Only local connections are allowed.
Please see https://chromedriver.chromium.org/security-considerations for suggestions on keeping ChromeDriver safe.
ChromeDriver was started successfully.
Sep 10, 2020 4:07:11 PM org.openqa.selenium.remote.ProtocolHandshake createSession
INFO: Detected dialect: W3C

*** THE TEST ENVIRONMENT DETAILS ARE CHROME||WINDOWS||LOCAL||Selenium Version is3.141.59||Session ID=2a130dc669feafb2fd360d97b32e4a87

After init
Before click
After click
UserName is: chaubalpinakin@gmail.com
Password is: Pc9121975!
Login button clicked
UserName verified
Pinakin Chaubal

  Scenario: To verify user name on Homepage                              # D:/pinakin.chaubal/workspace/cucumberpom/src/test/resources/featurefiles/HappyFlowFeaturePF.feature:3
    Given The user opens the "chrome" browser on "windows" and "local"  # LandingStepDefPF.i_open_the_browser_on_and(String,String,String)
    When The user navigates to the landing page                         # LandingStepDefPF.user_navigates_to_the_landing_page()
    And The user clicks the Login button on the landing page            # LandingStepDefPF.The_user_clicks_the_Login_button_on_the_landing_page()
    And The user enters "chaubalpinakin@gmail.com" as username          # LoginStepDefPF.user_enters_admin_as_username(String)
    And The user enters "Pc9121975!" as password                        # LoginStepDefPF.user_enters_admin_as_password(String)
    And The user clicks the Login button                                # LoginStepDefPF.user_clicks_the_Login_button()
    Then The user should be shown "Pinakin Chaubal" on top left corner  # HomePageStepDefPF.user_should_be_shown_User_Name_on_top_left_corner(String)

1 Scenarios (1 passed)
7 Steps (7 passed)
1m3.327s
```

Figure 6.2: Output of running Happy Flow with Page Factory

Finally, we will see an annotation that can be useful to speed up the test execution by caching the Web Elements. This annotation is the **`@CacheLookup`** annotation used in the Step Definitions.

6.10 Understanding the @CacheLookup annotation

`The @FindBy` annotation does the following when used in a Step Definition:

1. Navigates to the Document Object Model.
2. Searches for the element.
3. Initializes the element.
4. The element is ready for operations such as **`click().`**

There are many operations that are performed on WebElements and in a big project, there can be hundreds or even thousands of such WebElements. This increases the test execution time and reduces productivity.

To tackle this situation, Cucumber provides us with the **`@CacheLookup`** annotation. This annotation, when applied over a WebElement, instructs Selenium to maintain this WebElement in the Cache. Every Time afterwards, when an operation is performed on that particular WebElement, the element is picked from the Cache, thus saving the execution time.

The way we apply this annotation in the Page Object classes is shown as follows:

```
@CacheLookup
```

```
@FindBy(how=How.XPATH,using="//div[@role='listbox']")
public WebElement logOutDiv;
```

We will use **@CacheLookup** in all our Page Objects as we proceed to the remaining chapters.

With this, we come to the end of this chapter. We covered all concepts related to the Page Object Model with Page Factory.

Conclusion

This chapter covered the concept of the Page Object Model with PageFactory using Java. We started by understanding what the Page Factory Design Pattern is. We saw what the **PageFactory** class is. We learned about the **@FindBy**, **@FindBys**, and **@FindAll** annotations. We also learned about the **initElements()** static method of the **PageFactory** class. We looked at how our PageFactory will be designed. We designed our Login Scenario with the help of a Feature file. We created separate classes for the Locators using **@FindBy**. We then jumped into the main code for the Pages when we designed our Page Objects using composition. With the composition technique, we added the Page Locator class names inside the respective Page Objects and defined variables of that type. Eventually, we created the individual Step Definitions. Finally, we took a look at the **@CacheLookup** annotation used for improving the performance by speeding up the test execution by means of Caching the WebElement.

In the next chapter, we will take a look at how to configure the TestNG framework. This will be the start of Part-3. We will see how to configure the TestNG plugin in Eclipse. We will see how to convert the project to a TESTNG project and configure the **TestNG.XML** file. We will then execute the Runner class from TestNG XML.

Questions

1. Explain a Page Object Model with PageFactory.
2. Explain with an example the '@FindBy' annotation.
3. Explain with an example the '@FindBys' annotation.
4. Explain with an example the '@FindAll' annotation.
5. Create a Page Factory framework for logging into **www.gmail.com** and verifying the UserName.
6. Explain the @CacheLookup annotation.

CHAPTER 7
Configuring the TestNG Framework

In *Chapter 6, Learning about the Page Object Model using Page Factory,* we learned how to design page objects and used them in the Page Object Model framework with Page Factory. We learned the theory behind the Page Factory Design pattern and then learned about the **`Page Factory`** class. We learned about the **`@FindBy`** annotation and the related annotations, namely, **`@FindBys`** and **`@FindAll`**. We then looked at the **`initElements()`** method which is used for initializing the elements in the Page Factory. We looked at the design of the Page Factory framework and designed a Feature file for our Login Scenario. A separate Java class was created for locators of the three AUT pages covered by our scenario. We made use of the **`@FindBy`** annotation to create the locators. We then created an Abstract Base Page followed by the three child classes corresponding to the three AUT pages. These three java classes inherited the Abstract Base Page class. We used the concept of composition to include the Page Locator classes inside the Page Objects. We finally took a look at the **`@CacheLookup`** annotation which uses the concept of caching to improve the test execution performance.

In the first chapter of Part-3, we learned about the *TestNG* framework, which is a testing framework. We will take a look at how to configure the *TestNG* plugin in Eclipse. In *Chapter 1, Introduction to Behavior Driven Development,* we briefly touched upon the configuration of the *TestNG* plugin in Eclipse. We will look at the full procedure of how to configure *TestNG* as a plugin in Eclipse.

This chapter will make you an expert in designing a *TestNG* framework and invoking the Test Runner class created in *Chapter 4, Learning about the Test Runner*. By the end of this chapter we will have a *TestNG* framework that can be executed from an IDE.

The following topics will be covered in this chapter:

- Introduction to the TestNG framework
- Configuring the TestNG framework in Eclipse
- Glimpse of the TestNG XML from *Chapter 4*
- Various annotations in TestNG
- Executing the Test Runner from the TestNG XML

Objectives

After reading this chapter, the reader will be able to:

- Understand the TestNG framework
- One-time configuration of TestNG in Eclipse IDE
- Understand what goes in a TestNG XML
- Create a TestNG XML from scratch
- Use the various annotations as per need
- Execute the Test Runner from a TestNG XML

7.1 Introduction to the TestNG framework

TestNG is a test automation framework where NG represents the next **`generation.`** **`TestNG`** is a combination of JUnit (in Java) and NUnit (in C#). It is frequently used for unit, functional, integration, and end-to-end testing. TestNG has become very popular in the test automation area within a short time and has become one of the most widely used testing frameworks among developers (both application and test automation developers). It mainly uses annotations in Java to configure and write test methods.

TestNG was introduced by Cedric Beust. He developed it to overcome shortcomings in JUnit. A few of the features of TestNG are as follows:

- Additional before and after annotations like **`@BeforeTest`**, **`@AfterTest`**
- **`@BeforeClass`**, **`@AfterClass`**
- Grouping test methods by creating TestNG groups
- Incorporating dependencies using **`dependsOn`**

- Executing tests in parallel
- Basic test execution reporting

TestNG is a testing framework which is written in Java and can be used with Java and also with Java-related languages such as Groovy. In TestNG, suites and tests are configured through the use of XML files. By default, the name of this file is **testng.xml,** but it can be given another name if need be.

TestNG enables us to do test configuration through XML files and allows us to include (or exclude) respective packages, classes, and methods in the test suite. It also allows users to group test methods into particular named groups, which can be included or excluded as part of the test execution.

Parameterization of test methods is easy using TestNG, and it also provides the facility of creating data-driven tests.

TestNG has exposed its API, which has made it easy to add custom functionalities or extensions if required.

7.2 Configuring the TestNG framework in Eclipse

In *Chapter 1: Introduction to Behavior Driven Development, section 1.9,* we covered the configuration of TestNG in Eclipse using Eclipse MarketPlace. In this section, we will see a different method of configuring TestNG in Eclipse. Apart from this, we will add the TestNG jar to **POM.XML**. Let's start with the Maven configuration.

Add the dependency shown as follows to the **POM.XML:**

```
<!-- https://mvnrepository.com/artifact/org.testng/testng -->
<dependency>
<groupId>org.testng</groupId>
<artifactId>testng</artifactId>
<version>6.14.3</version>
<scope>test</scope>
</dependency>
```

After adding this dependency, right click on the project->**Maven | Update Project.**

Let's now see how to configure the **TestNG** Plugin in Eclipse using a different approach.

Follow the given steps to install the *TestNG* Plugin:

1. Go to **`Help | Install New Software.`**
2. Input **'http://dl.bintray.com/testng-team/testng-eclipse-release/'** in the '*Work with:*' text box. Click on the check box next to TestNG and click on **`Next`**.

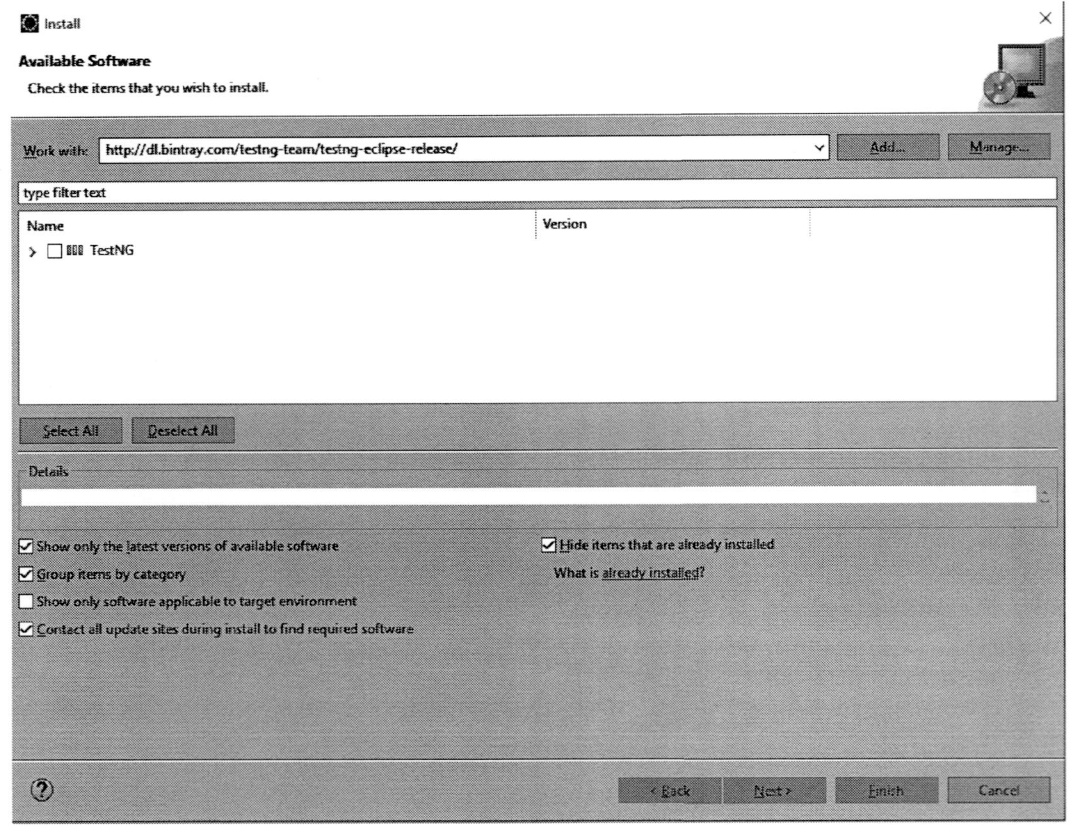

Figure 7.1: *Installing the TestNG plugin in Eclipse*

3. Since we already installed the plugin in *Chapter 1, Introduction to Behavior Driven Development*, we get the message as shown in the following screenshot:

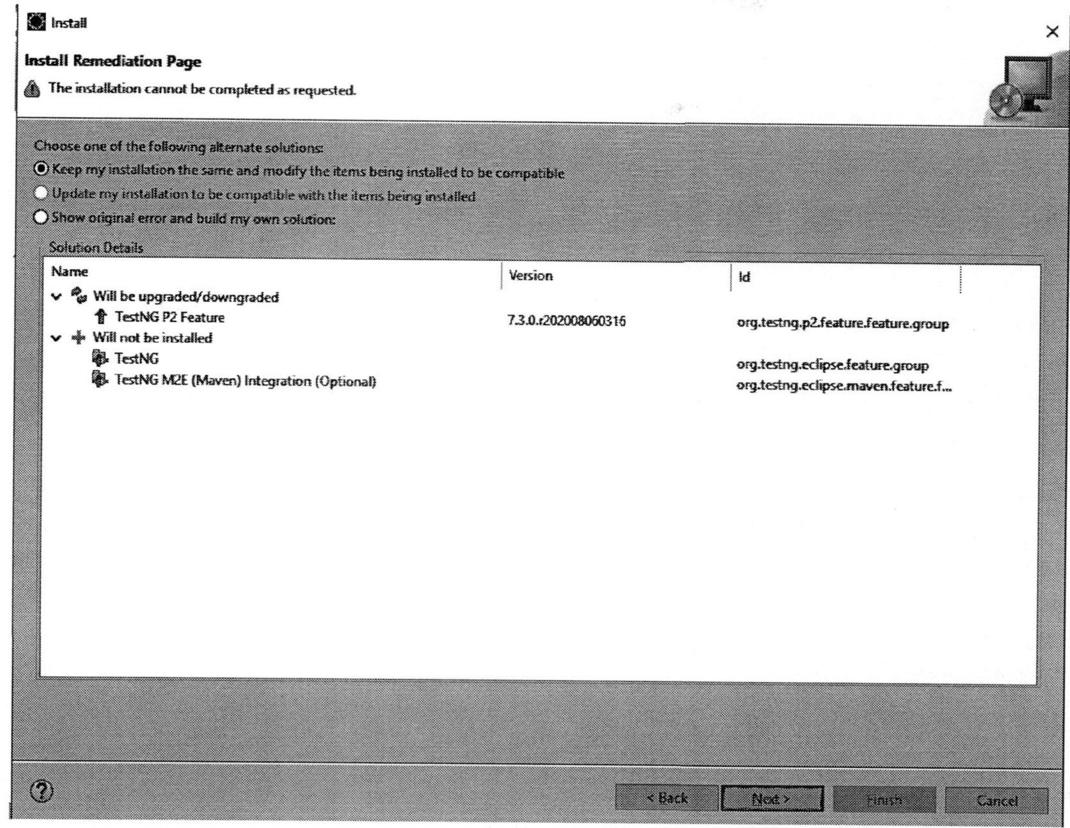

Figure 7.2: Installation already exists

Click on the **`Cancel`** button here. This is another way to install the *TestNG* Plugin in Eclipse.

Right click on the project and click on **`TestNG | Convert to TestNG`** if you have not done so already in *Chapter 1, Introduction to Behavior Driven Development, Section 1.9.*

7.3 Glimpse of the TestNG XML

In *Chapter 4: Learning about the Test Runner, section 4.6,* we took a look at the TestNG Runner class and the '**`testng.xml`**' file that got generated when we right clicked on the project and did a **`TestNG | Convert to TestNG.`** Let's take a closer look at this xml file:

```
<?xml version="1.0" encoding="UTF-8"?>

<!DOCTYPE suite SYSTEM "http://testng.org/testng-1.0.dtd">

<suite name="Suite">

  <test thread-count="5" name="Test">
```

```
    <classes>
      <class name="testrunner.BPBTR_1"/>
    </classes>
  </test> <!-- Test -->
</suite> <!-- Suite -->
```

Here, we have a '**Suite**' tag and inside this tag, we have a test tag with a thread-count parameter that tells us how many threads would be created when this TestNG XML is executed. In the preceding example, we create 5 threads which can be executed in parallel. As we build upon this TestNG XML, we will get introduced to a few more parameters.

Next, let's take a look at the various annotations provided by TestNG.

7.4 Various annotations in TestNG

Let's take a look at the various annotations that we have used in our **Test Runner** class:

- **@BeforeClass**

  The method annotated with this annotation gets executed before any test method in the current class.

- **@AfterClass**

  The method annotated with this annotation gets executed after all test methods in the current class have been invoked.

- @Test

  The method / methods annotated with this annotation gets executed as a part of the test.

- @DataProvider

  The method annotated with this annotation is useful for providing test data to the methods annotated as '**@Test(dataProvider="features")**'. The data provider method itself has an annotation of '**@DataProvider**' and an optional name.

7.5 A look at the updated HomePage pageobject and step definitions

We have made some minor code modifications in the Homepage page object and step definition. Let's first take a look at the HomePage page object.

We made the '**verifyUser()**' method return a Homepage object and we captured that returned object in an object of the Homepage page object.

Here is the **verifyUser()** method. Notice how we are returning the same HomePage object:

```
public HomepagePF verifyUser(String userDisplayText) {
        Assert.assertEquals(homepageLocators.userDisplay.getText(),
userDisplayText);
        return new HomepagePF();
}
```

We capture the returned object in an object of type HomepagePF in the Step Definition and then use the same object to invoke the **LogOut()** method in the Homepage which has been changed as follows:

```
public void logOut() {
homepageLocators.logOutDiv.click();
        homepageLocators.logOutSpan.click();
}
```

We modified the **tearDown()** method as follows and placed it in the **@AfterHook** class **BPBSD_99**. Now, this method only has the **close()** and **quit()** methods for the driver object:

```
@After
public void tearDown() {
        SingletonDriver.getInstance().getDrvr().close();
        SingletonDriver.getInstance().getDrvr().quit();


}
```

The updated Step Definition Java class is shown as follows. Here, we capture the returned Homepage object in a **HomePage** variable as follows:

```
public class HomePageStepDefPF {
        HomepagePF homePagePF = new HomepagePF();
        @Then("^The user should be shown \"(.*?)\" on top left corner$")
        public void user_should_be_shown_User_Name_on_top_left_
corner(String
                                userDisplayText) throws Throwable {
            System.out.println("UserName verified");
```

```
            homePagePF = homePagePF.verifyUser(userDisplayText);
            homePagePF.logOut();
      }
}
```

After the Logout happens, the method annotated with **@After** executes, which simply closes and quits the browser:

```
public class BPBSD_99 {

      @After
      public void tearDown() {
            System.out.println("In teardown");
            SingletonDriver.getInstance().getDrvr().close();
            SingletonDriver.getInstance().getDrvr().quit();

      }

}
```

After these changes, we can execute our **TestRunner** class using **TestNG.xml**.

7.6 Executing the Test Runner from the TestNG XML

To execute the **TestRunner** class from Eclipse, right click on the testng xml and select '**Run As | TestNG Suite**. We get the output as shown in the following screenshot:

```
*** THE TEST ENVIRONMENT DETAILS ARE CHROME||WINDOWS||LOCAL||Selenium Version is3.141.59||Session ID=64b648bbf09395d9f2d2352ea2e1ae8a

After init
Before click
After click
UserName is: chaubalpinakin@gmail.com
Password is: Pc9121975!
Login button clicked
UserName verified
In teardown

  Scenario: To verify user name on Homepage                    ⊠[90m# HappyFlowFeaturePF.feature:4⊠[0m
    ⊠[32mGiven ⊠[0m⊠[32mThe user opens the "⊠[0m⊠[32m⊠[1mchrome⊠[0m⊠[32m" browser on "⊠[0m⊠[32m⊠[1mwindows⊠[0m⊠[32m" and "⊠[0m⊠[32m⊠[1mlocal⊠[0m⊠[32m"⊠[0m ⊠[90m# LandingStepDefPF.i_c
    ⊠[32mWhen ⊠[0m⊠[32mThe user navigates to the landing page⊠[0m                ⊠[90m# LandingStepDefPF.user_navigates_to_the_landing_page()⊠[0m
    ⊠[32mAnd ⊠[0m⊠[32mThe user clicks the Login button on the landing page⊠[0m      ⊠[90m# LandingStepDefPF.The_user_clicks_the_Login_button_on_the_landing_page()⊠[0m
    ⊠[32mAnd ⊠[0m⊠[32mThe user enters "⊠[0m⊠[32m⊠[1mchaubalpinakin@gmail.com⊠[0m⊠[32m" as username⊠[0m      ⊠[90m# LoginStepDefPF.user_enters_admin_as_username(String)⊠[0m
    ⊠[32mAnd ⊠[0m⊠[32mThe user enters "⊠[0m⊠[32m⊠[1mPc9121975!⊠[0m⊠[32m" as password⊠[0m                ⊠[90m# LoginStepDefPF.user_enters_admin_as_password(String)⊠[0m
    ⊠[32mAnd ⊠[0m⊠[32mThe user clicks the Login button⊠[0m                ⊠[90m# LoginStepDefPF.user_clicks_the_Login_button()⊠[0m
    ⊠[32mThen ⊠[0m⊠[32mThe user should be shown "⊠[0m⊠[32m⊠[1mPinakin Chaubal⊠[0m⊠[32m" on top left corner⊠[0m ⊠[90m# HomePageStepDefPF.user_should_be_shown_User_Name_on_top_left_cor

1 Scenarios (⊠[32m1 passed⊠[0m)
7 Steps (⊠[32m7 passed⊠[0m)
0m25.578s


0 Scenarios
0 Steps
0m0.000s


===============================================
Suite
Total tests run: 1, Failures: 0, Skips: 0
===============================================
```

Figure 7.3: Running the TestNG suite

We can see that the browser quits due to the presence of the AfterHook.

We come to the end of the chapter on TestNG configuration in Eclipse. We saw how we can execute our Cucumber Test Runner with the help of TestNG xml.

Conclusion

This chapter covered the TestNG configuration in Eclipse and we also saw how to execute the project from **`testng.xml`**. We introduced the **`@AfterHook`** back into the BPBSD_99 Step Definition. This is the single place where we need to mention this After Hook annotation. We made the **`logOut()`** method specific to the Log out steps and the Driver close and Quit code was put in the After Hook class BPBSD_99. We made the **`verifyUser()`** method of the **`HomepagePF`** page object return an object of the **`HomepagePF`** class and captured it in a variable of type HomepagePF. Thus, when we call the **`LogOut`** functionality in the **`HomepagePF`** class from the Step Definition, it does not throw a null pointer.

In the next chapter *'Configuring Maven and Learning about POM.XML'*, we will take a look at configuring Maven and the POM Xml. We will learn about the Maven Surefire plugin. We will run our build from **`pom.xml`** which in turn will trigger the TestNG XML and our framework.

Questions

1. Explain what a TestNG framework is.
2. How do you convert a project to TestNG?
3. Explain with an example the various annotations of TestNG.
4. Explain with an example the @Test annotation.
5. Try running the code from TestNG xml.

Chapter 8
Configuring Maven and Learning About POM.xml

In *Chapter 7, Configuring the TestNG framework,* we learned how to configure the TestNG framework. We got introduced to the TestNG framework and learned how to configure the TestNG framework in Eclipse IDE. We looked at the TestNG xml which we used for triggering our tests through the Test Runner class. We also looked at the various annotations that were used in the Test Runner class. We learned how to execute the **TestRunner** class from our TestNG xml.

In this chapter, we learn about the Maven build tool. We will start with the installation part. We will take a look at what group ID and artifact ID mean in Maven. We will take a look at concepts such as dependencies, the build tag, and how to configure plugins. We will learn about the *'Maven Compiler Plugin'* and *'Maven Surefire Plugin'* and the configuration tag. We will take a look at the Maven build phases.

This chapter will help you understand Maven. By the end of this chapter, the reader will be able to understand Maven as a build tool.

The following topics will be covered in this chapter:

- Downloading and installing Maven
- Configuring M2_HOME and path environment variables
- Understanding Maven Local and Central repositories

- Learning about Maven build lifecycle phases and goals
- Understanding the pom.xml
- Learning about Maven profiles
- Adding a new Maven profile
- Learning the important Maven plugins
- Dependency management in Maven

Objectives

After reading this chapter, the reader will be able to:

- Download and install Maven
- Understand one-time configuration of environment variables for Maven
- Understand Maven repositories and build phases
- Understand the `pom.xml` file
- Learn about Maven profiles and add a new profile
- Learn about the important Maven plug-ins
- Learn about dependency management

Apache Maven is a popular tool for automating software projects, mainly Java projects and is also used for building Selenium projects. Maven addresses two aspects of the software build process. It specifies how a software is built and also describes its dependencies. Maven uses convention over configuration for the build process. An XML file also known as pom.xml (**pom** stands for **Project Object Model**) describes the software project that is being built, its dependencies on other modules or components, directories, the build order, and necessary plugins. It comes with predefined targets to perform tasks, such as code compilation and packaging. Maven dynamically downloads Maven plugins and Java libraries from one or more online repositories, such as the **Maven Central Repository**, and stores them locally in the Local Repository.

Let's take the first step towards Maven by downloading and installing it.

8.1 Downloading and extracting Maven

We will cover the Maven download process for Windows. The prerequisites for Maven installation are as follows:

- Java should be installed [Preferably version 1.8]. Make sure the JDK is present.

- **`The JAVA_HOME`** environment variable should be configured.
- Path to the **`bin`** folder of Java should be configured in the path environment variable.

Navigate to **http://maven.apache.org** and download the zip file corresponding to the latest stable release. Extract it to a convenient location. Once extracted, the folder structure should include the folders mentioned as follows:

- **`bin`**: This contains the required files to run Maven on different platforms.
- **`conf`**: This contains the settings.xml file which can be used to configure certain Maven settings.
- **`boot`**: This contains the required jar files for Maven to start.
- **`lib`**: This contains the libraries used by Maven along with an **`ext`** folder which contains third-party extensions to change the default Maven implementation.

Once Maven is downloaded and extracted, we need to add a new environment variable and edit the '**`path`**' Environment variable.

8.2 Configuring M2_HOME and path environment variables

Now that Maven is downloaded and extracted, let's add the **`M2_HOME`** environment variable as follows:

1. Open **`Control Panel | All Control Panel Items | System on the computer.`**
2. Choose Advanced system settings.
3. Click on '**`Environment Variables`**'.
4. Add the **`M2_HOME`** environment variable and set its value to the folder where Maven was extracted.
5. Edit the path environment variable and append Maven installation's bin folder path.

Verify that the Maven installation is proper by opening the Command Prompt and type the following command:

```
mvn -version
```

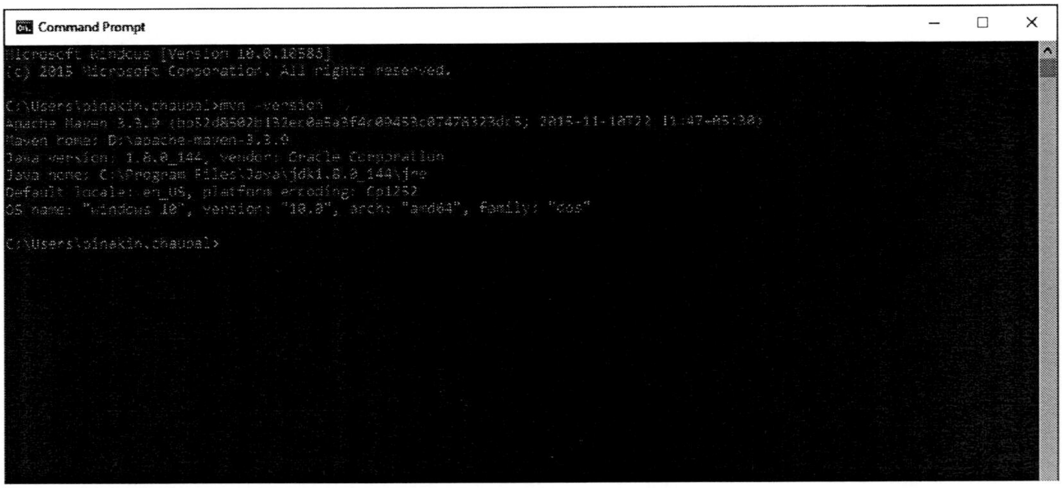

***Figure 8.1**: Checking the Maven installation*

If the text similar to the preceding screenshot gets displayed, we are sure that Maven has been installed successfully. Now that Maven is installed, let's start understanding concepts related to Maven. We will begin by understanding the repository concept in Maven.

8.3 Understanding Maven local and central repositories

A repository in Maven is a physical directory that contains JAR files along with meta data about the JAR files. The meta data is in the form of POM files which has project information and other external dependencies that the JAR file has. There are two kinds of repositories, namely, Local and Central.

Let's understand the difference between the two:

- **Local Repository**: This resides on the developer's machine in **`C:\Users\pinakin.chaubal\.m2\repository.`**
- **Central Repository**: This is located at **https://maven.apache.org/repository/index.html**. When a Maven build job is run, Maven tries to locate the dependency in the local repository and if it is unable to find the dependency in the local repository, the dependency gets downloaded from the Central Repository into the **`.m2`** folder mentioned above.

When we learn about the POM XML file, we will see how to mention dependencies of the project along with the versions. Let's learn a little about the build phases in Maven.

8.4 Learning about Maven build lifecycle phases and goals

Maven is based on the concept of a build lifecycle where the process of building and distributing a particular artifact is defined clearly. The person in charge of the project build has to know only a limited number of commands to run a Maven project and the POM file takes care of getting this done for us. There are three build lifecycles that are built in, namely, default, clean, and site. A brief description of the three build lifecycles is given as follows:

- **default lifecycle**: This handles the project deployment.
- **clean lifecycle**: This handles the project cleaning.
- **site lifecycle**: This handles the project's site documentation.

Each build lifecycle is defined by a different list of build phases. A build phase is nothing but a stage in the lifecycle. As an example, let's consider the default lifecycle which comprises the following phases:

- **Validate**: The project is validated for correctness and availability of necessary information.
- **Compile**: This is used for compilation of the source code of the project.
- **Test**: The compiled source code is tested using a unit testing framework like TestNG or Junit.
- **Package**: The compiled code is packaged into a distributable format like JAR.
- **Verify**: Checks are run on the results of integration tests to ensure quality of deliverables.
- **Install**: The package is installed in the local repository so that it can be used as a dependency for other projects locally.
- **Deploy**: This is done in the build environment where the final package is copied to the remote repository so that it can be used by other projects.

In our case, when we say 'mvn test', the **validate** and **compile** phases get executed before the **test** phase. The default lifecycle phases get executed in order, starting from **validate** and ending at the desired phase.

Let's understand the concept of plugin goals.

A plugin goal represents a task which is fine grained than a build phase and contributes to the building and managing of a project. It may be bound to either zero or more build phases. A goal that is not bound to any build phase can be executed independently outside the build lifecycle through direct invocation.

Let's take a look at the **`pom.xml`** in detail.

8.5 Understanding the pom.xml

In this section, we will understand what the **`pom.xml`** file is and what goes into it. **POM** stands for **Project Object Model** and the **`pom.xml`** is used for configurations of a Maven Project. The pom.xml file is based on a specific schema as indicated in the '**`project`**' tag shown as follows:

```
<project xmlns="http://maven.apache.org/POM/4.0.0" xmlns:xsi="http://
www.w3.org/2001/XMLSchema-instance" xsi:schemaLocation="http://maven.
apache.org/POM/4.0.0 http://maven.apache.org/xsd/maven-4.0.0.xsd">
```

The version of the schema is indicated in the '**`modelVersion`**' tag as follows:

```
<modelVersion>4.0.0</modelVersion>
```

The group ID is indicated by the **`groupId`** tag and it is a unique ID for the organization indicated as a reverse domain name as follows:

```
<groupId>bpb.cucumber</groupId>
```

The artifact ID indicates the name of the project as follows:

```
<artifactId>cucumberpom</artifactId>
```

The version tag relates to the specific instance of our project. 'SNAPSHOT' indicates that this is work in progress:

```
<version>0.0.1-SNAPSHOT</version>
```

The build tag specifies the plugins to be used in the project. In our case, we have two plugins specified in the **`POM.XML`** file, namely, the **Maven Compiler Plugin** and **Maven Surefire** plugin.

The dependencies tag specifies all the external dependencies in the form of JAR files required for the project. These dependencies are downloaded automatically when the pom file is saved.

That is all that is needed to know about the POM file as far as our framework is concerned. Let's now learn about Maven profiles.

8.6 Learning about Maven profiles

A portable build is one that works on different platforms and runtime environments. Profiles can be used to build the same project in a different manner depending on the platform and environment. In order to view Maven profiles, open the file '**settings.xml**' in the **conf** folder as shown in the following screenshot:

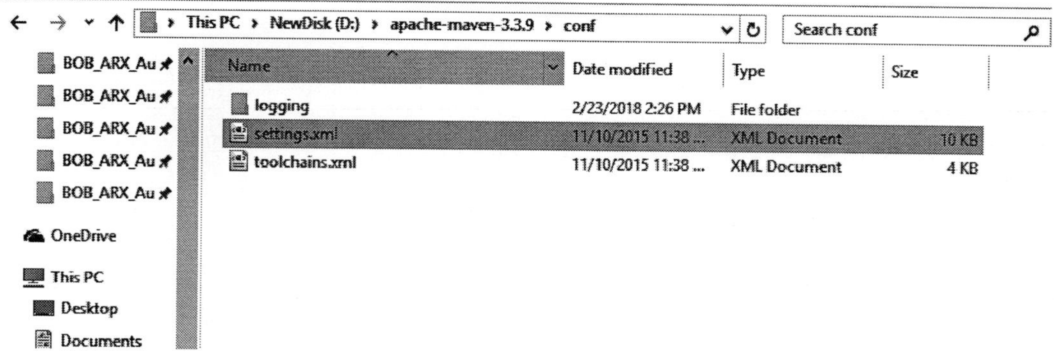

Figure 8.2: *The settings.xml file in Maven folder*

View the Profile tag that is commented in the file is shown as follows:

```
<profile>
  <id>env-dev</id>
  <activation>
    <property>
      <name>target-env</name>
      <value>dev</value>
    </property>
  </activation>
  <properties>
    <tomcatPath>/path/to/tomcat/instance</tomcatPath>
  </properties>
</profile>
```

Maven provides us with the following three types of profiles:

- Global profile defined in the **settings.xml** in the Maven home directory.
- Per project profile defined in the pom file of the project.
- Per user profile defined in the user settings in the **.m2** folder under the User's home folder.

Let's take a look at how to add a new profile.

8.7 Adding a new Maven profile

In the pom file under your project, add the code as follows:

```
<profiles>
      <profile>
          <id>sit</id>
          <activation>
              <activeByDefault>false</activeByDefault>
          </activation>
      </profile>
 </profiles>
```

There are two ways to create a profile. In the Setting xml file or project's pom file, if there is an active profile in the **settings.xml**, it will override the profile with equivalent IDs in the pom file.

Let us now see two important Maven plugins that we will be using in our project.

8.8 Learning the important Maven plugins

The two important plugins that we will use are shown as follows:

1. **Maven Compiler Plugin**: Compilation is a very important step performed by any build tool. Maven makes use of the Maven compiler plugin to do the compilation. To use the Maven compiler plugin, run the following command on the project that we have created till now:

   ```
   mvn compile
   ```

   This command will compile the source files present in the project. The following text gets displayed in the command prompt window. Since all

Java classes are already compiled, we will get the output as shown in the following screenshot:

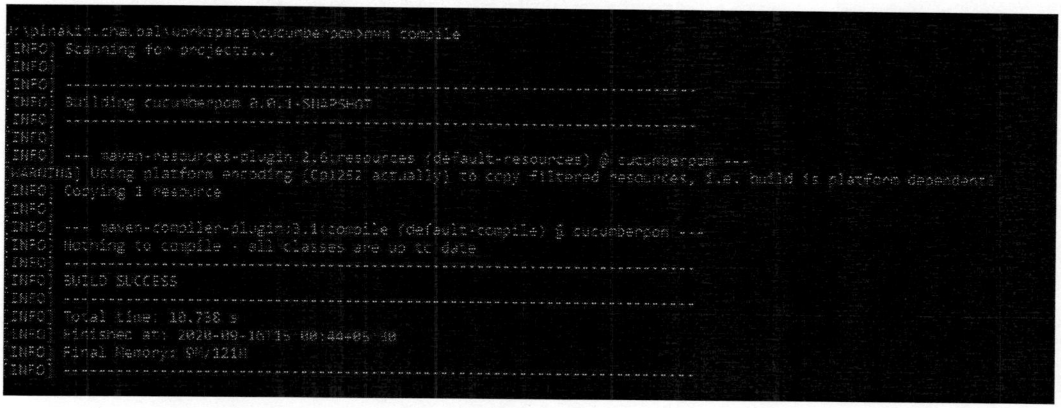

```
:\pinakin.chaubal\workspace\cucumberpom>mvn compile
[INFO] Scanning for projects...
[INFO]
[INFO] ------------------------------------------------------------------------
[INFO] Building cucumberpom 0.0.1-SNAPSHOT
[INFO] ------------------------------------------------------------------------
[INFO]
[INFO] --- maven-resources-plugin:2.6:resources (default-resources) @ cucumberpom ---
[WARNING] Using platform encoding (Cp1252 actually) to copy filtered resources, i.e. build is platform dependent!
[INFO] Copying 1 resource
[INFO]
[INFO] --- maven-compiler-plugin:3.1:compile (default-compile) @ cucumberpom ---
[INFO] Nothing to compile - all classes are up to date
[INFO] ------------------------------------------------------------------------
[INFO] BUILD SUCCESS
[INFO] ------------------------------------------------------------------------
[INFO] Total time: 10.738 s
[INFO] Finished at: 2020-09-16T15:00:44+05:30
[INFO] Final Memory: 9M/121M
[INFO] ------------------------------------------------------------------------
```

***Figure 8.3**: Compiling a project using Maven Compiler plugin*

The Maven compiler plugin is mentioned in the POM xml shown as follows. This snippet will be put under the **<plugins>** tag that comes under the **<build>** tag. Notice that we are mentioning the Java source and target versions as **1.8**:

```
<plugin>
        <groupId>org.apache.maven.plugins</groupId>
        <artifactId>maven-compiler-plugin</artifactId>
        <version>3.1</version>
        <configuration>
                <source>1.8</source>
                <target>1.8</target>
        </configuration>
</plugin>
```

Let's take a look at the Maven Surefire plugin next.

2. **Maven Surefire Plugin**: We will utilize the Maven Surefire plugin to execute our TestNG tests in the upcoming chapter. Add the following plugin in **pom.xml**. Note how we have mentioned '**testng.xml**' in the **<suiteXmlFile>** tag:

```
<plugin>
        <groupId>org.apache.maven.plugins</groupId>
        <artifactId>maven-surefire-plugin</artifactId>
        <version>2.19.1</version>
```

```
                    <configuration>
                          <suiteXmlFiles>
                                <suiteXmlFile>testng.xml</suiteXmlFile>
                          </suiteXmlFiles>
                    </configuration>
              </plugin>
```

Let's see what dependency management in Maven is all about.

8.9 Dependency management in Maven

One of the prominent features of Maven is managing the dependencies required by a particular project. A project always or most of the time depends on other executables or dependencies. The typical issues faced while using dependencies are related to the choice of dependencies, the versions, and the transitive dependencies (a dependency being dependent on other dependencies).

The way we specify dependencies in a pom file is by mentioning a **<dependency>** tag inside the **<dependencies>** tag is shown as follows:

```
<dependencies>
<!-- https://mvnrepository.com/artifact/info.cukes/cucumber-java -->
    <dependency>
           <groupId>io.cucumber</groupId>
           <artifactId>cucumber-java</artifactId>
           <version>6.10.3</version>
    </dependency>
</dependencies>
```

Here, we are mentioning the dependency for cucumber-java where the version is 1.2.4. Maven looks into the local repository first to see whether the jar with the specified version exists. If it does not exist, then it is downloaded from the Maven central repository to the local repository.

Conclusion

This chapter covered the Maven build tool and explored important concepts related to the Maven build tool. We started off with downloading and installing Maven from the Maven website. We configured the M2_HOME and path environment variables. We understood the difference between Maven central and local repositories. We looked at the build lifecycle, phases, and goals. We learned about the structure of `pom.xml`. We also learned about Maven profiles and how to add a Maven profile. We got introduced to the Maven Compiler plugin and Maven Surefire plugin. Finally, we took a look at Dependency Management in Maven.

In the next chapter '*Test execution with Maven and Log4J*', we will take a look at how we can execute the Compile from Eclipse as well as Command Line. In addition to this, we will see how we can implement Logging in the framework using the *Log4J* framework. We will create a separate class for generating logs.

Questions

1. Explain the difference between Maven central and local repositories.
2. Explain the Maven lifecycle phases.
3. Explain the meaning of goals in Maven.
4. What is a Maven profile and how to add a Maven profile?
5. Explain dependency management in Maven.

Chapter 9
Test Execution with Maven and Log4J

In *Chapter 8, Configuring Maven and learning about POM.xml,* we learned about downloading and installing Maven. We configured the M2_HOME and the path environment variables. We looked at what Maven local and central repositories are. We learned about Maven lifecycle phases and goals. We took a look at the **`pom.xml`**. We learned about Maven profiles and how to add a new Maven profile. We looked at important Maven plugins and dependency management in Maven.

In this chapter, we will learn about the project execution with Maven and with the command line. We will just compile the project with maven using the command line. We will also create a class for logging and then create an object of this class in all Page Object classes. We will then log statements to the console. We will also create a log file with the log statements. We will have a clean framework ready where we can view the logging statements.

This chapter will make you understand the execution of the project from Eclipse and the command line with Maven. The reader will understand how to create a generic logging class which can be used by other classes for logging purpose.

Structure

The following topics will be covered in this chapter:

- Understanding the Log4J framework

- Creating a generic class for logging
- Creating a log4j properties file
- Invoking the custom logger from the page objects
- Compiling the project with Eclipse
- Compiling the project from the command line

Objectives

After reading this chapter, the reader will be able to:

- Understand the Log4J framework
- Create a generic logger for logging purpose
- Create the log4j.properties file
- Call this custom logger from the Page objects
- Execute the compile from Eclipse
- Execute the compile from the command line

Logging in any automation framework is an important activity. It gives the test engineer information on what happened in the test execution since most of the time, tests get executed in off hours. Through logging, the engineer can figure out the line number and the module in case of failures in the test execution.

Let's understand the Log4J framework which we will use for logging in test automation.

9.1 Understand the Log4J framework

Log4J is a logging framework written in Java that is used for generating logs during test execution.

Log4J is configurable through external configuration files which can be either xml or property files. In order to use Log4J, the log4J dependency should be added to the **pom.xml** as follows:

```
<!-- https://mvnrepository.com/artifact/log4j/log4j -->
<dependency>
<groupId>log4j</groupId>
<artifactId>log4j</artifactId>
<version>1.2.17</version>
```

```
</dependency>
```

After including this dependency, right click on the project and select **Maven | Update Project**. The required JAR files will be downloaded in the **.m2** folder.

Log4J has three main components listed as follows:

- **Loggers**: This is used for capturing logging information.
- **Appenders**: This is used for redirecting logging information to various preferred destinations [like Console or File Systems].
- **Layouts**: This is used for formatting logging information in different styles.

Let's understand the steps involved in using Log4J to log user-defined output statements in the code.

9.2 Create a generic class for logging

For logging information to the console and file, we will use a user-defined class. This will be a very simple class as follows.

Create a class called **LoggerUtil.java** in the package **utils** in **src/main/java** as follows:

```
package utils;
import org.apache.log4j.Logger;
import org.apache.log4j.PropertyConfigurator;
public class LoggerUtil {
private static boolean customRoot=false;
      public static Logger getCustomLogger(Class mycls){
            if(customRoot){
                  return Logger.getLogger(mycls);
            }
            PropertyConfigurator.configure("log4j.properties");
            customRoot = true;
            return Logger.getLogger(mycls);
      }
}
```

The preceding **LoggerUtil** class defines a static Boolean variable called **customRoot**. If the root logger for Log4J has been already created by any class in the framework, the logger for that class will be returned else a new logger gets created.

Let's move to the **log4j.properties** file creation.

9.2.1 Create a log4j.properties file

Along with this class, we should have the **log4j.properties** file at the root of the project.

The contents of the **log4j.properties** is shown as follows:

```
# Define custom root logger with file appender. Level of the root logger is defined as INFO
log4j.rootLogger = INFO, FILE, stdout

# Define the FILE Appender, the threshhold, the layout and the
# conversion #pattern
# The logging levels are in the order ALL(Integer.MAX_VALUE)
# <TRACE(600) < #DEBUG(500) < #INFO(400) < WARN(300) < ERROR(200) <
# FATAL(100) < OFF(0). Since we #have kept the logging #level # at
# INFO here, all INFO,WARN,ERROR,FATAL messages #will be displayed.
# The DEBUG and #TRACE level messages are not displayed

log4j.appender.FILE=org.apache.log4j.FileAppender
log4j.appender.FILE.File=automationtest.out
log4j.appender.FILE.MaxFileSize=20MB
log4j.appender.FILE.MaxBackupIndex=5
log4j.appender.FILE.Append=true
log4j.appender.FILE.layout=org.apache.log4j.PatternLayout
log4j.appender.FILE.layout.ConversionPattern=%d{yyyy-MM-dd HH:MM:SS} %-5p %c{1}:%L - %m%n
log4j.appender.FILE.Threshold=INFO

# This will print log in console
log4j.appender.stdout=org.apache.log4j.ConsoleAppender
log4j.appender.stdout.Target=System.out
log4j.appender.stdout.layout=org.apache.log4j.PatternLayout
log4j.appender.stdout.layout.ConversionPattern=%d{yyyy-MM-dd HH:MM:SS} %-5p %c{1} :%L - %m%n
log4j.appender.stdout.Threshold=INFO
```

The log messages will be pushed to the **`automationtest.out`** file, which will be appended every. On reaching 20 MB, a new file gets created. The new file will be an archived version, and at the place where it shows the type, the version number will be listed. For example, the first file will be of type 1 and the second of type 2. When the version 2 file is created, the version 1 file data will be pushed to version 2, and the current version data will be pushed to version 1. The next thing worth mentioning is that there can be only five versions that can be created, as indicated by MaxBackupIndex. After the fifth version, once **`maxFileSize`** is reached, data will start flowing from the current version to version 1, from version 1 to version 2, version 2 to version 3, and so on. Data in version 5 that was originally there will be overwritten by data from version 4.

Another point to note is about the logging levels. Logging levels are used to categorize entries in log files. This categorization is done based on urgency. Using logging levels one can manage the information that is logged. There are 8 logging levels which are listed as follows:

- **ALL**: This turns on all levels of logging.
- **DEBUG**: This is used for debugging. Messages appear in log files once this level is set.
- **INFO**: This is used to record messages about routine operations of the application.
- **WARN**: This is used to indicate that an error exists in the system.
- **ERROR**: This indicates a serious problem that requires immediate attention.
- **FATAL**: This indicates a very serious problem which might result in a system crash if not addressed immediately.
- **OFF**: This turns off logging.
- **TRACE**: This is introduced in version 1.2 and adds more information to DEBUG level logs.

Let's see how we can invoke this custom logger from our page objects.

9.3 Invoke the custom logger from the page objects

In order to invoke the custom logger from the page objects, we need to get the logger for the respective class from the **`CustomLogger`** class and then use the **`info(String)`** method wherever required. Here is the sample code that has to be included in the page objects.

Perform the following steps:

1. Include the following line of code as the first line in the Page Object classes:

```
Logger logger = LoggerUtil.getCustomLogger(LoginPagePF.class);
```

2. Include logging statements wherever necessary in the code as follows:

```
public void enterUserName(String userName) {
            logger.info("Entering username");
            loginpageLocators.email.sendKeys(userName);
      }
```

Now, we will just compile the project from Eclipse and the command line.

9.4 Compile from Eclipse

Now that we have our Custom Logger in place, let's see how to compile the project from Eclipse. When we right click on the project in Eclipse and select **`Run As | Maven Install,`** we get the output similar to the one shown in the following screenshot:

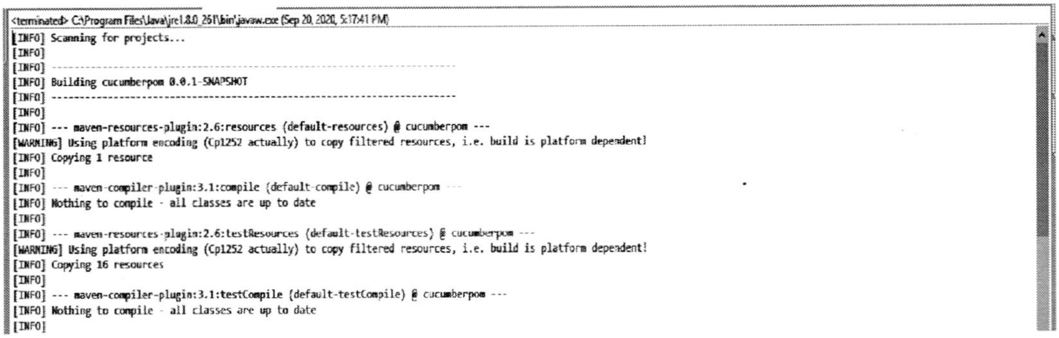

```
<terminated> C:\Program Files\Java\jre1.8.0_261\bin\javaw.exe (Sep 20, 2020, 5:17:41 PM)
[INFO] Scanning for projects...
[INFO]
[INFO] ------------------------------------------------------------------------
[INFO] Building cucumberpom 0.0.1-SNAPSHOT
[INFO] ------------------------------------------------------------------------
[INFO]
[INFO] --- maven-resources-plugin:2.6:resources (default-resources) @ cucumberpom ---
[WARNING] Using platform encoding (Cp1252 actually) to copy filtered resources, i.e. build is platform dependent!
[INFO] Copying 1 resource
[INFO]
[INFO] --- maven-compiler-plugin:3.1:compile (default-compile) @ cucumberpom ---
[INFO] Nothing to compile - all classes are up to date
[INFO]
[INFO] --- maven-resources-plugin:2.6:testResources (default-testResources) @ cucumberpom ---
[WARNING] Using platform encoding (Cp1252 actually) to copy filtered resources, i.e. build is platform dependent!
[INFO] Copying 16 resources
[INFO]
[INFO] --- maven-compiler-plugin:3.1:testCompile (default-testCompile) @ cucumberpom ---
[INFO] Nothing to compile - all classes are up to date
[INFO]
```

Figure 9.1: Console output in Eclipse

We will see our Custom Logger in action in the next chapter when we take a look the Maven Surefire plugin in detail.

9.5 Executing the Compile from the command line

We will now prepare our Command Line to execute the framework. Open the framework and navigate to the framework directory. Type '**`mvn install`**'.

The command line shows the output as shown in the following screenshot:

```
D:\sinakin.chauhal\workspace\cucumberpom>mvn install
[INFO] Scanning for projects...
[INFO]
[INFO] ------------------------------------------------------------------------
[INFO] Building cucumberpom 0.0.1-SNAPSHOT
[INFO] ------------------------------------------------------------------------
[INFO]
[INFO] --- maven-resources-plugin:2.6:resources (default-resources) @ cucumberpom ---
[WARNING] Using platform encoding (Cp1252 actually) to copy filtered resources, i.e. build is platform dependent!
[INFO] Copying 1 resource
[INFO]
[INFO] --- maven-compiler-plugin:3.1:compile (default-compile) @ cucumberpom ---
[INFO] Nothing to compile - all classes are up to date
[INFO]
[INFO] --- maven-resources-plugin:2.6:testResources (default-testResources) @ cucumberpom ---
[WARNING] Using platform encoding (Cp1252 actually) to copy filtered resources, i.e. build is platform dependent!
[INFO] Copying 16 resources
[INFO]
[INFO] --- maven-compiler-plugin:3.1:testCompile (default-testCompile) @ cucumberpom ---
[INFO] Nothing to compile - all classes are up to date
```

Figure 9.2: *Console output on Command Line*

If there are any compile errors, those will get listed here.

This brings us to the end of this chapter.

Conclusion

This chapter covered the logging framework Log4J and the installation procedure for Log4J. We added the required dependency in the pom.xml and took a look at how to create a custom Log4J logger class. We then took a look at the log4j.properties file which is the configuration file for Log4J. We then added the logger object in our page objects and added logging statements in the three page objects. We looked at executing the compile from Eclipse and the command line.

In the next chapter *'Configuring pom.xml to trigger TestNG.xml'*, we will take a look at using the Maven Surefire plugin to execute our feature files. We will also get to see the console output of Log4J. Eventually, we will take a look at the output file from Log4J.

Questions

1. Explain the Log4J framework and its uses.
2. Create a sample Logger class.
3. Explain the process of creating and using the Logger object.
4. Write a simple compile in the pom.xml file.
5. Execute the compile from Eclipse and the Command Line.

Chapter 10
Configuring POM.XML to Trigger TestNG.XML

In the previous chapter, we learned about the Log4J framework and what goes in the **`log4j.properties`** for the configuration of Log4J. We then created a custom Logger class for generating logs in our framework. We then used the Logger object from this class to display logs in the console and a log file with the extension '**`.log`**'. We also learned about the concept of **`MaxFileSize`** and **`MaxBackupIndex`**. We then invoked the **`customLogger`** class method **`getLogger()`** to fetch a Logger and used the **`info()`** method to display logs. Eventually, we saw the execution of the project with Maven.

In this chapter, we will learn about the Surefire plugin and see how we can use the plugin to execute tests from the TestNG xml. Our TestNG XML executes the TestRunner which executes the feature files with specific tags. We will configure the Maven Surefire plugin to trigger the TestNG XML which in turn will trigger the TestRunner class. The TestRunner class executes the Feature files based on tags.

This chapter will make you understand the execution of the TestNG xml from the **`pom.xml`** using the Maven Surefire plugin. We will also take a look at the Surefire reports that get generated after the run.

Structure

The following topics will be covered in this chapter:

- Understanding the Maven Surefire plugin
- Configuring the pom for using the Surefire plugin
- Executing the **pom.xml** and the tests from Eclipse
- Executing the tests with Maven from the command line
- Examining the Surefire reports
- Skipping tests

Objectives

After reading this chapter, the reader will be able to:

- Learn about the Maven Surefire plugin.
- Learn the configuration of the pom for using the Surefire plugin.
- Execute the **pom.xml** and the tests from Eclipse.
- Execute the **pom.xml** and the tests from the Command Line.
- Examining the **index.html** and the Emailable report.
- How to skip tests.

Executing tests is the heart of the framework. We have executed tests in the previous chapters using the **testng.xml**. Instead of running the TestNG xml directly, we will invoke the TestNG xml from the pom xml using the Surefire plugin.

Let's understand the Surefire plugin which we will use for executing the **TestNG.xml**.

10.1 Understand the Maven Surefire plugin

The Surefire plugin is used during the test phase of the build lifecycle to execute the unit tests of an application. It generates reports in two different file formats for normal Java programs:

- Plain text files (*.txt)
- XML files (*.xml)

By default, these files are generated in **${basedir}/target/surefire-reports/TEST-*.xml**.

Let's see how to use the Suite XML files for executing TestNG xml next.

10.2 Configure the pom for using the Surefire plugin

In order to use TestNG suite XML files such as the testng xml, a Surefire plugin with the configuration shown below should be added. This allows the flexible configuration of the tests to be run. Add the xml snippet to the **pom.xml** in the **<plugins></plugins>** tags as follows:

```
<plugin>
        <groupId>org.apache.maven.plugins</groupId>
        <artifactId>maven-surefire-plugin</artifactId>
        <version>2.14.1</version>
        <configuration>
                <suiteXmlFiles>
                        <suiteXmlFile>testng.xml</suiteXmlFile>
                </suiteXmlFiles>
        </configuration>
</plugin>
```

In the preceding configuration, the **testng.xml** should be at the same level as the **pom.xml**. The **testng.xml** file is specified within a **<suiteXmlFiles>** tag.

When we take a look at parallel execution using Maven and TestNG, we will revisit the Surefire plugin in order to understand a few more parameters.

The Maven Surefire plugin can also be used with JUnit but using the Surefire plugin with JUnit is out of scope of this book.

Now, we are ready to execute our **testng.xml** from with the **pom.xml** using the Maven Surefire plugin.

10.3 Executing the pom.xml and the tests from Eclipse

Open the Eclipse IDE, right click on the **`Project`** and select **`Run As | Maven Install`** as shown in the following screenshot:

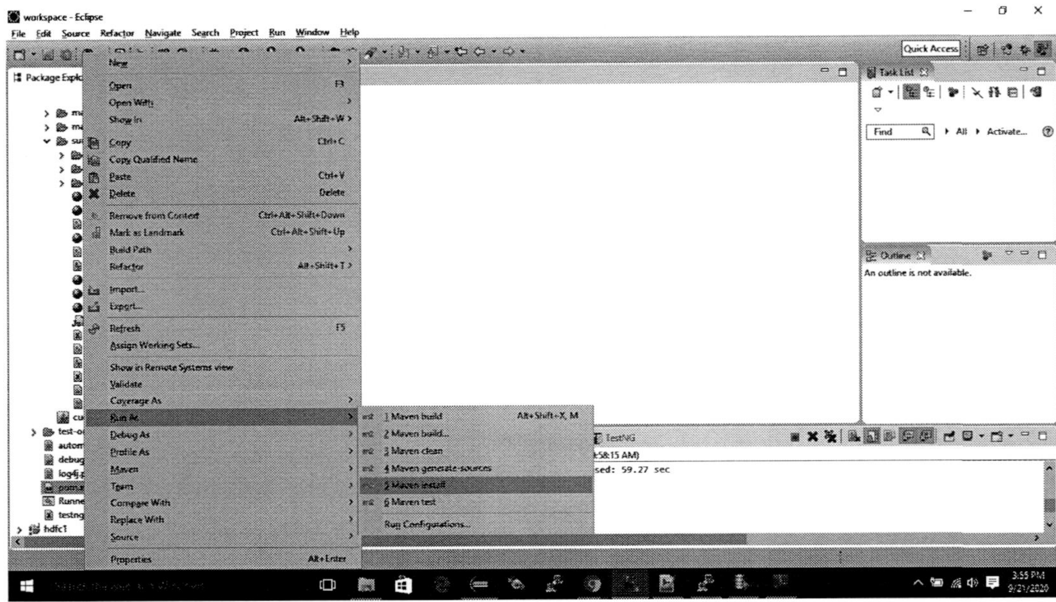

Figure 10.1: *Executing POM as Maven Install*

The tests get executed as per the tags in the **`testng.xml`**. The console output in Eclipse is shown in the following screenshot:

```
[INFO] --- maven-install-plugin:2.4:install (default-install) @ cucumberpom ---
[INFO] Installing D:\pinakin.chaubal\workspace\cucumberpom\target\cucumberpom-0.0.1-SNAPSHOT.jar to C:\Users\pinakin.chaubal\.m2\repository\bpb\cucumber\cucumberpom\0.0.1-SNAPSHOT\cu
[INFO] Installing D:\pinakin.chaubal\workspace\cucumberpom\pom.xml to C:\Users\pinakin.chaubal\.m2\repository\bpb\cucumber\cucumberpom\0.0.1-SNAPSHOT\cucumberpom-0.0.1-SNAPSHOT.pom
[INFO] ------------------------------------------------------------------------
[INFO] BUILD SUCCESS
[INFO] ------------------------------------------------------------------------
[INFO] Total time: 01:13 min
[INFO] Finished at: 2020-09-21T09:59:31+05:30
[INFO] Final Memory: 12M/88M
[INFO] ------------------------------------------------------------------------
```

Figure 10.2: *Successful test execution*

The log statements in the code that were introduced in the previous chapter are displayed in the console output in Eclipse as shown in the following screenshot:

```
*** THE TEST ENVIRONMENT DETAILS ARE CHROME||WINDOWS||LOCAL||Selenium Version is3.141.59||Session ID=ecc82dc82606ac08b829feb8270267ea

2020-09-21 09:09:379 INFO  LandingPagePF :26 - Clicking Login button on Landing page
UserName is: chaubalpinakin@gmail.com
2020-09-21 09:09:269 INFO  LoginPagePF :21 - Entering username
Password is: Pc9121975!
2020-09-21 09:09:736 INFO  LoginPagePF :25 - Entering password
Login button clicked
2020-09-21 09:09:37 INFO  LoginPagePF :29 - Clicking Login button on Login screen
UserName verified
2020-09-21 09:09:366 INFO  HomepagePF :26 - Verifying user text
2020-09-21 09:09:14 INFO  HomepagePF :32 - Clicking Logout Div
2020-09-21 09:09:158 INFO  HomepagePF :34 - Clicking Logout Span
After all methods
In teardown

  Scenario: To verify user name on Homepage                  ⊠[90m# HappyFlowFeaturePF.feature:4⊠[0m
    ⊠[32mGiven ⊠[0m⊠[32mThe user opens the "⊠[0m⊠[32m⊠[1mchrome⊠[0m⊠[32m" browser on "⊠[0m⊠[32m⊠[1mwindows⊠[0m⊠[32m" and "⊠[0m⊠[32m⊠[1mlocal⊠[0m⊠[32m"⊠[0m ⊠[90m# LandingStepDefPF.i_c
    ⊠[32mWhen ⊠[0m⊠[32mThe user navigates to the landing page⊠[0m          ⊠[90m# LandingStepDefPF.user_navigates_to_the_landing_page()⊠[0m
    ⊠[32mAnd ⊠[0m⊠[32mThe user clicks the Login button on the landing page⊠[0m     ⊠[90m# LandingStepDefPF.The_user_clicks_the_Login_button_on_the_landing_page()⊠[0m
    ⊠[32mAnd ⊠[0m⊠[32mThe user enters "⊠[0m⊠[32m⊠[1mchaubalpinakin@gmail.com⊠[0m⊠[32m" as username⊠[0m      ⊠[90m# LoginStepDefPF.user_enters_admin_as_username(String)⊠[0m
    ⊠[32mAnd ⊠[0m⊠[32mThe user enters "⊠[0m⊠[32m⊠[1mPc9121975!⊠[0m⊠[32m" as password⊠[0m      ⊠[90m# LoginStepDefPF.user_enters_admin_as_password(String)⊠[0m
    ⊠[32mAnd ⊠[0m⊠[32mThe user clicks the Login button⊠[0m          ⊠[90m# LoginStepDefPF.user_clicks_the_Login_button()⊠[0m
    ⊠[32mThen ⊠[0m⊠[32mThe user should be shown "⊠[0m⊠[32m⊠[1mPinakin Chaubal⊠[0m⊠[32m" on top left corner⊠[0m ⊠[90m# HomePageStepDefPF.user_should_be_shown_User_Name_on_top_left_cor

1 Scenarios (⊠[32m1 passed⊠[0m)
7 Steps (⊠[32m7 passed⊠[0m)
0m57.609s

Tests run: 1, Failures: 0, Errors: 0, Skipped: 0, Time elapsed: 59.27 sec

Results :

Tests run: 1, Failures: 0, Errors: 0, Skipped: 0
```

Figure 10.3: Displaying Logger output

Executing Maven Install from Eclipse is ok as far as the verification of test results during the test development phase is concerned. We are going to integrate our project with Jenkins in the upcoming chapters and that requires us to execute the framework from the Command Line.

10.4 Executing the pom.xml and the tests from the Command Line

Let us now see how to execute the `MVN Install` command from the Command Prompt. When we trigger this command after navigating to the project directory, we get the console output as shown in the following screenshot:

Figure 10.4: Successful command line execution

We also get the Log4J statements as follows. We can see that the console output from Eclipse is the same as the console output from the command line execution:

Figure 10.5: Displaying Logger statements

Now that we have executed the test, it is time to see what all reports have been generated from the test. With TestNG in picture, we have TestNG specific reports.

Let's take a look at the reports that got generated.

10.5 Examining the Surefire reports

We will see the following two reports that will be of use to analyze test results:

- `Index.html` report
- Emailable report

The **`Index.html`** report is a comparatively simple report that gives basic information like the Test Runner name, the feature description, and the passed methods on the tests being run as shown in the following screenshot:

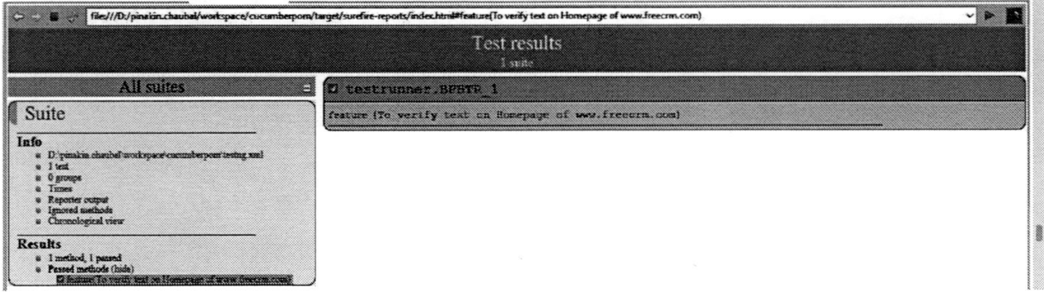

Figure 10.6: Index.html report

There is another report known as the Emailable report that one can send in an email to the Senior Management. This report gives a little more insight on the test execution.

The Emailable report is shown as follows. The Emailable report has systematic information about the tests being run along with the passed/failed/skipped status. It gives the Suite/Test status as shown in the following screenshot:

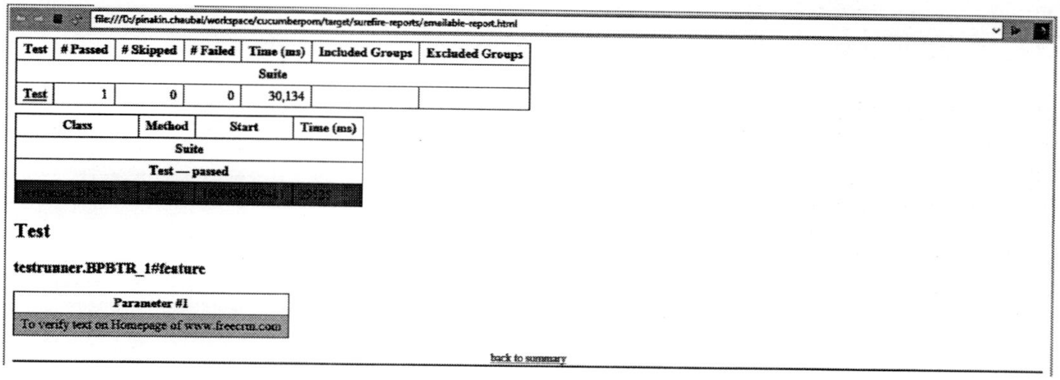

file:///D:/pinakin.chaubal/workspace/cucumberpom/target/surefire-reports/emailable-report.html

Test	# Passed	# Skipped	# Failed	Time (ms)	Included Groups	Excluded Groups
Suite						
Test	1	0	0	30,134		

Class	Method	Start	Time (ms)
Suite			
Test — passed			
[illegible]	[illegible]	[illegible]	[illegible]

Test

testrunner.BPBTR_1#feature

Parameter #1
To verify text on Homepage of www.freecrm.com

back to summary

Figure 10.7: Emailable report for Management

10.6 Skipping Tests

There might be situations where the tests should not be executed. The probable reason for this might be that few tests are broken. This can be achieved by including the tag **`<skipTests>`**.. When the value of this tag is set to true, none of the tests will get executed:

```
<plugin>
        <groupId>org.apache.maven.plugins</groupId>
        <artifactId>maven-surefire-plugin</artifactId>
        <version>2.14.1</version>
        <configuration>
                <suiteXmlFiles>
                        <suiteXmlFile>testng.xml</suiteXmlFile>
                </suiteXmlFiles>
                <skipTests>true</skipTests>
        </configuration>
</plugin>
```

After making the change, right click on **pom.xml** and select **Run As | Maven Install**. The console output states that none of the tests were executed as shown in the following screenshot:

```
<terminated> C:\Program Files\Java\jre1.8.0_261\bin\javaw.exe (Sep 21, 2020, 5:01:02 PM)
[INFO] Scanning for projects...
[INFO]
[INFO] ------------------------------------------------------------------------
[INFO] Building cucumberpom 0.0.1-SNAPSHOT
[INFO] ------------------------------------------------------------------------
[INFO]
[INFO] --- maven-resources-plugin:2.6:resources (default-resources) @ cucumberpom ---
[WARNING] Using platform encoding (Cp1252 actually) to copy filtered resources, i.e. build is platform dependent!
[INFO] Copying 1 resource
[INFO]
[INFO] --- maven-compiler-plugin:3.1:compile (default-compile) @ cucumberpom ---
[INFO] Nothing to compile - all classes are up to date
[INFO]
[INFO] --- maven-resources-plugin:2.6:testResources (default-testResources) @ cucumberpom ---
[WARNING] Using platform encoding (Cp1252 actually) to copy filtered resources, i.e. build is platform dependent!
[INFO] Copying 16 resources
[INFO]
[INFO] --- maven-compiler-plugin:3.1:testCompile (default-testCompile) @ cucumberpom ---
[INFO] Nothing to compile - all classes are up to date
[INFO]
[INFO] --- maven-surefire-plugin:2.14.1:test (default-test) @ cucumberpom ---
[INFO] Tests are skipped.
[INFO]
[INFO] --- maven-jar-plugin:2.4:jar (default-jar) @ cucumberpom ---
[INFO] Building jar: D:\pinakin.chaubal\workspace\cucumberpom\target\cucumberpom-0.0.1-SNAPSHOT.jar
[INFO]
[INFO] --- maven-cucumber-reporting:2.8.0:generate (execution) @ cucumberpom ---
```

***Figure 10.8**: Skipping Tests*

This was a comparatively short chapter which showed us how we can make use of the Surefire plugin to execute the TestNG xml file.

Conclusion

This chapter covered a plugin called '*Maven Surefire Plugin*' which we used to execute the **testng.xml** files. For this, we made use of **<suiteXmlFile>** in which we mentioned the name of the testng xml file which invokes the Test Runner class. The Test Runner has tags which execute Feature files with respective tags. We configured the POM xml using the **<suiteXmlFile>** tag in the Surefire plugin. We then executed the tests from the Eclipse IDE and the Command Line. We then examined the index and Emailable reports generated by the test run. We eventually looked at how to skip tests if the tests are broken.

In the next chapter '*Configuring the Runner for Cucumber JVM Reports,*' we will take a look at configuring the Runner class to generate the Cucumber JVM reports. We will get to see statistical reports which provide better information on the test execution.

Questions

1. Explain the Maven Surefire plugin.
2. List the various tags in the Maven Surefire plugin.
3. Create a TestNG xml and execute it from pom.xml using the Surefire plugin.
4. Execute the test and generate the index.html and Emailable report.
5. Execute the Maven install command with skipping tests.

CHAPTER 11
Configuring the Runner Class for the Cucumber Reporter Plugin

In *Chapter 10, Configuring POM.XML to trigger TestNG.XML,* we looked at the **`Maven Surefire`** plugin. This plugin was used to trigger the TestNG xml file from within the POM xml file. The **`<suiteXmlFile>`** tag was used for this purpose. Within this tag, we just had the name of the TestNG xml which is **`testng.xml`**. There was no absolute or relative path mentioned for the testng xml since the TestNG xml is at the same level as the pom xml file. We executed our test from Eclipse first by right clicking on the project and clicking on **`Run As | Maven Install`**. We then opened the command prompt and navigated to the project directory. We executed the command **`mvn install`** and the test ran in the same manner as it did from the Eclipse IDE.

In this chapter, we learn about the **`<testFailureIgnore>`** tag. We will add a plugin called the **`maven-cucumber-reporting`** plugin which we will use for generating beautiful HTML reports. We will create one positive scenario and one negative scenario in the first feature file and one negative scenario in the second feature file and place the same tag on both the feature files. We will modify the test runner class so that it is able to generate Cucumber JVM reports. The scenarios get executed in a serial fashion generating a report for each feature file.

This chapter will help you understand the configuration of the Test Runner class for generating the Cucumber JVM reports. After reading this chapter, the reader will understand how to generate feature files with multiple scenarios and then generate a consolidated report for the execution of these feature files.

Structure

The following topics will be covered in this chapter:

- Understanding the `<testFailureIgnore>` tag
- Understand the maven-cucumber-reporting plugin
- Capturing screenshots of failed scenario steps
- Modifying the Test Runner for Cucumber JVM reports
- Creating Feature files with multiple scenarios
- Changing the modules related to the Home Page
- Executing the multiple feature files with the help of tags
- Examining the Cucumber-JVM reports

Objectives

After reading this chapter, the reader will be able to:

- Get familiar with the `<testFailureIgnore>` tag
- Learn about the `maven-cucumber-reporting` plugin
- Capture screenshots of failed scenario steps
- Modify the Test Runner class
- Create a Feature file with multiple scenarios
- Execute the multiple feature files with the help of tags
- Examine the Cucumber-JVM reports

Let's start by understanding the `<testFailureIgnore>` tag of the *Maven Surefire* plugin which will help in the continuation of the test execution even if scenarios fail.

11.1 Understanding the <testFailureIgnore> tag

On occasions where there are hundreds of tests to be executed, we may want to continue execution even if few of the tests fail. The feature file design should be such that the tests are mutually independent of each other and can execute without a dependency on other feature files. The `<testFailureIgnore>` tag helps to ignore failures in the test execution and move to the next scenario. The scenario design should be such that each of the scenarios should be a complete one. If a scenario opens a browser window, then the same scenario should close the browser window so that the next scenario starts afresh without stale browser sessions.

The xml fragment from the POM xml is shown as follows:

```
<plugin>
<groupId>org.apache.maven.plugins</groupId>
      <artifactId>maven-surefire-plugin</artifactId>
      <version>2.14.1</version>
      <configuration>
            <suiteXmlFiles>
                  <suiteXmlFile>testng.xml</suiteXmlFile>
            </suiteXmlFiles>
            <skipTests>false</skipTests>
            <testFailureIgnore>true</testFailureIgnore>
      </configuration>
  </plugin>
```

As shown in the preceding code, we will ignore test failures in our test execution so that all scenarios in all the feature files get executed and we get a consolidated output.

11.2 Understand the maven-cucumber-reporting plugin

This chapter is about the Cucumber JVM reports for which we need to configure a plugin called the **maven-cucumber-reporter** plugin. This plugin will help in the generation of the Cucumber JVM reports. The plugin is shown as follows:

```
      <plugin>
            <groupId>net.masterthought</groupId>
            <artifactId>maven-cucumber-reporting</artifactId>
            <version>2.8.0</version>
            <executions>
            <execution>
      <id>execution</id>
      <phase>verify</phase>
      <goals>
```

```
                <goal>generate</goal>
                </goals>
                <configuration>
                <projectName>cucumberpom</projectName>
                <!-- optional, per documentation set this to "true" to
bypass generation of Cucumber Reports entirely, defaults to false if not
specified -->
                <skip>false</skip>
                <!-- output directory for the generated report -->
                <outputDirectory>target/cucumber-reports/advanced-
reports</outputDirectory>
                <cucumberOutput>target/cucumber-reports</cucumberOutput>
                <inputDirectory>${project.build.directory}/cucumber-
reports</inputDirectory>
                     <jsonFiles>
                         <param>**/*.json</param>
                </jsonFiles>
                <enableFlashCharts>true</enableFlashCharts>

                </configuration>
             </execution>
          </executions>
       </plugin>
```

The main tags to note in this plugin are listed as follows:

- **Execution**: This gives the details of what exactly has to be executed. The phase is specified as 'verify' and the goal is specified as generate. We will run '**`mvn install`**' which will automatically run the verify and use the generate goal to create the reports.
- **Configuration** - The report directory location is mentioned in the configuration section. The JSON output once created will be placed at the location specified in the **`<cucumberOutput>`** tag and the Cucumber JVM reports will be placed at the location specified in **`<outputDirectory>`**. The JSON files that should be picked up for generating the reports are mentioned in the **`<jsonFiles>`** tag.

Now that we have the reporting plugin set up, we will see how we can capture the screenshot for failed scenario steps and embed within the scenario so that we can view the screenshot in the JVM report.

11.3 Capturing screenshots of failed scenario steps

A very common practice in test automation is capturing screenshots when a failure occurs. Selenium provides us with the **TakesScreenshot** interface and the **getScreenshotAs()** method. The TakesScreenshot interface is used for capturing the screenshot and storing it in a specified location. We will capture the screenshot of the entire page. After taking the screenshot, it needs to be stored somewhere at a convenient location. Cucumber provides the embed(byte[], String) method for embedding the screenshot directly into the Cucumber JVM report. The screenshot is stored in a **byte** array which is then passed to the embed method which places the screenshot in the Cucumber JVM report.

We will place the method for taking screenshots on failure in the method annotated with **@After** so that it runs at the end of the scenario. The After Hook is shown as follows:

```
package stepdefinitions;

import org.openqa.selenium.OutputType;
import org.openqa.selenium.TakesScreenshot;

import cucumber.api.Scenario;
import cucumber.api.java.After;
import locators.HomepageLocators;
import pageobjects.AbstractBasePage;
import singletondriver.SingletonDriver;
import utils.Assertions;

public class BPBSD_99 {

	@After
	public void tearDown(Scenario scenario) {
		if (scenario.isFailed()) {
			byte[] screenPrint = ((TakesScreenshot)
SingletonDriver.getInstance().getDrvr()).getScreenshotAs(OutputType.
BYTES);
			scenario.embed(screenPrint, "image/png");
		}

		try {
```

```
                    if (!(SingletonDriver.getInstance().
getSessId()==null)) {
                    SingletonDriver.getInstance().getDrvr().close();
                    SingletonDriver.getInstance().getDrvr().quit();
                    }
              } catch (Exception e) {
                          e.printStackTrace();
              }

       }

}
```

We will take a look at the output when we verify the JVM report.

11.4 Modifying the Test Runner for Cucumber JVM reports

Till now we have been using a Test Runner with **@BeforeClass**, **@Test**, **@ DataProvider,** and **@AfterClass** annotations. Now onwards, we will use a simpler version of the TestRunner (**BPBTR_2.java**) as follows:

```
package testrunner;


import cucumber.api.CucumberOptions;
import cucumber.api.testng.AbstractTestNGCucumberTests;


@CucumberOptions(features = { "src/test/resources/featurefiles" }, glue =
{ "stepdefinitions" }, plugin = {
                    "pretty", "json:target/cucumber-reports/cucumber-
test.json" }, tags = {"@Sanity1"})


public class BPBTR_2 extends AbstractTestNGCucumberTests {


}
```

We still extend the Runner class with **AbstractTestNGCucumberTests** in order to use TestNG. We also use the **@CucumberOptions** annotation that has the location of our feature file and step definitions. We will also specify the location of the json file that gets generated at the end of the execution. We have tags mentioned so that only feature files that have the tag as **`@Sanity1`** get executed.

Those are the changes that need to be done in the Test Runner. Let's go ahead and create test cases in the form of Feature files.

11.5 Creating Feature files with multiple scenarios

We will create two feature files. The conditions checked in the Feature files are given as follows:

1. **`HappyFlowFeaturePF.feature`:** This feature file will have a positive scenario followed by a negative scenario as shown in the following screenshot:

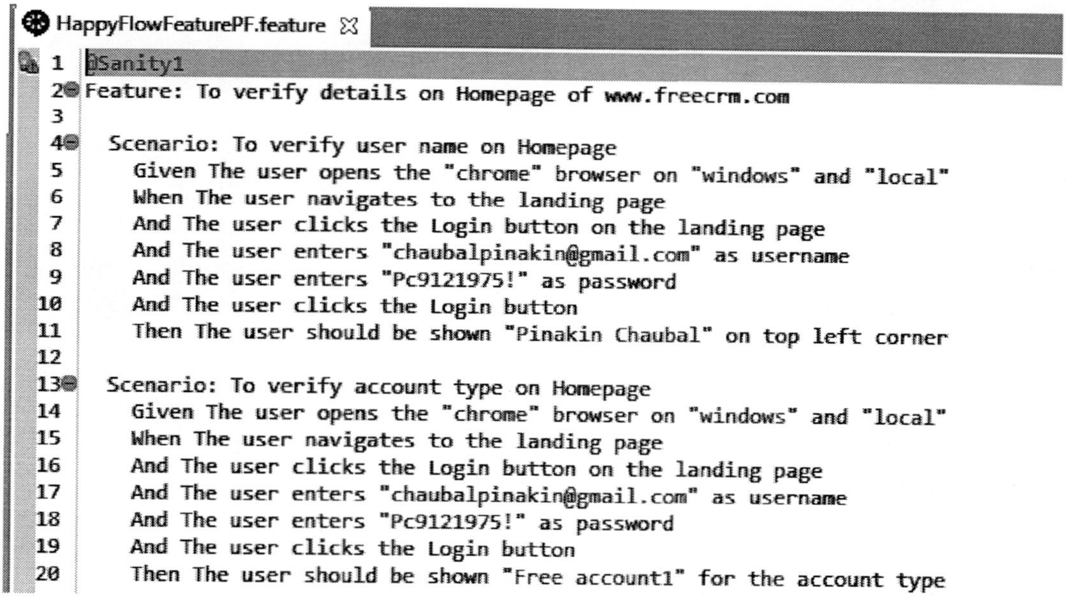

HappyFlowFeaturePF.feature

```
@Sanity1
Feature: To verify details on Homepage of www.freecrm.com

  Scenario: To verify user name on Homepage
    Given The user opens the "chrome" browser on "windows" and "local"
    When The user navigates to the landing page
    And The user clicks the Login button on the landing page
    And The user enters "chaubalpinakin@gmail.com" as username
    And The user enters "Pc9121975!" as password
    And The user clicks the Login button
    Then The user should be shown "Pinakin Chaubal" on top left corner

  Scenario: To verify account type on Homepage
    Given The user opens the "chrome" browser on "windows" and "local"
    When The user navigates to the landing page
    And The user clicks the Login button on the landing page
    And The user enters "chaubalpinakin@gmail.com" as username
    And The user enters "Pc9121975!" as password
    And The user clicks the Login button
    Then The user should be shown "Free account1" for the account type
```

***Figure 11.1**: Feature file with two scenarios*

We have kept the scenarios simple but data can be embedded in scenario data tables or scenario outline data tables if need be.

2. **HappyFlowFeatureNF.feature:** This feature file will have one negative scenario as shown in the following screenshot:

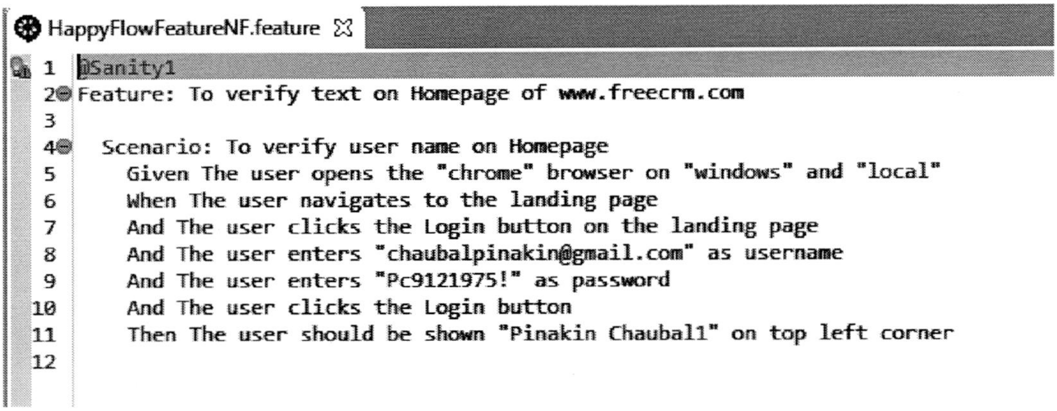

HappyFlowFeatureNF.feature

```
@Sanity1
Feature: To verify text on Homepage of www.freecrm.com

  Scenario: To verify user name on Homepage
    Given The user opens the "chrome" browser on "windows" and "local"
    When The user navigates to the landing page
    And The user clicks the Login button on the landing page
    And The user enters "chaubalpinakin@gmail.com" as username
    And The user enters "Pc9121975!" as password
    And The user clicks the Login button
    Then The user should be shown "Pinakin Chaubal1" on top left corner
```

Figure 11.2: Feature file with one scenario

Both the feature files will get executed one after another and two JVM reports get generated. As seen in the preceding screenshot, one new scenario for verifying the Account Type has been added. Now, we will see the changes that are needed when new scenarios which access different WebElements are introduced.

The account type is a WebElement on the home page and hence we will modify the **HomePageStepDefPF.java**, **HomepageLocators.java,** and **HomepagePF.java**.

11.6 Changing the modules related to Home Page

We have a new scenario for verifying the Account Type on the home page and this involves modifications in three Java classes. Let's see what changes are required.

11.6.1 Modifications in the HomepageLocators.java

Since we are going to check the Account Type on the Home Page, we need to add the locator for the Account Type web element as follows:

```
@FindBy(how=How.XPATH,using="//a[@href=\"/settings/billing/\"]")
public WebElement acctType;
```

We have used XPATH to locate the element. We will make use of the **href** attribute of the WebElement to create the locator.

We now see the modifications required in the **HomePageStepDef.java**.

11.6.2 Modifications in the HomePageStepDef.java

We will add the regular expression and the attached method to the **HomePageStepDef.java** so that it can handle the execution of the Scenario step. The method that needs to be added is shown as follows:

```
	@Then("^The user should be shown \"([^\"]*)\" for the account type$")
	public void the_user_should_be_shown_for_the_account_type(String acctType) throws Throwable {
		System.out.println("Account type verified");
		homePagePF = homePagePF.verifyAccountType(acctType);
		homePagePF.logOut();
	}
```

Note that all we do here invoke the **verifyAccountType** method from the Home Page page object class (**HomepagePF.java**). This method returns an object of the class **HomepagePF** which is captured in the object of type **HomepagePF** so that we can then use it to invoke the **logOut()** method from the **HomepagePF** class to log out gracefully.

11.7 Executing the multiple feature files with the help of tags

We will now execute the new Test Runner using the **pom.xml**. Right click on the **pom.xml** in Eclipse IDE and click on **Run As | Maven Install** or use "**mvn clean verify**" from the command line.

HappyFlowFeatureNF.feature is executed first. It fails with an assertion error for the **UserName** text as follows:

```
2021-05-28 08:05:397 INFO  LandingPagePF :26 - Clicking Login button on Landing page
UserName is: chaubalpinakin@gmail.com
2021-05-28 08:05:260 INFO  LoginPagePF :21 - Entering username
Password is: Pc9121975!
2021-05-28 08:05:749 INFO  LoginPagePF :25 - Entering password
Login button clicked
2021-05-28 08:05:318 INFO  LoginPagePF :29 - Clicking Login button on Login screen
UserName verified
2021-05-28 08:05:429 INFO  HomepagePF :30 - Verifying user text
In teardown
In teardown failure
```

Figure 11.3: *Console log output for HappyflowFeatureNF.feature*

The exact assertion failure is shown as follows:

```
[31mjava.lang.AssertionError: expected [Pinakin Chauball] but found [Pinakin Chaubal]
    at org.testng.Assert.fail(Assert.java:96)
    at org.testng.Assert.failNotEquals(Assert.java:776)
    at org.testng.Assert.assertEqualsImpl(Assert.java:137)
    at org.testng.Assert.assertEquals(Assert.java:118)
    at org.testng.Assert.assertEquals(Assert.java:453)
    at org.testng.Assert.assertEquals(Assert.java:463)
    at pageobjectspf.HomepagePF.verifyUser(HomepagePF.java:31)
    at stepdefinitions.HomePageStepDefPF.user_should_be_shown_User_Name_on_top_left_corner(HomePageStepDefPF.java:14)
    at ?.Then The user should be shown "Pinakin Chaubal1" on top left corner(HappyFlowFeatureNF.feature:11)
```

Figure 11.4: Assertion error for HappyflowFeatureNF.feature

`HappyFlowFeaturePF.feature` is executed next where the positive scenario of the UserName text verification is executed first. This is a successful execution with graceful logout.

```
2021-05-28 08:05:277 INFO  LandingPagePF :26 - Clicking Login button on Landing page
UserName is: chaubalpinakin@gmail.com
2021-05-28 08:05:162 INFO  LoginPagePF :21 - Entering username
Password is: Pc9121975!
2021-05-28 08:05:220 INFO  LoginPagePF :25 - Entering password
Login button clicked
2021-05-28 08:05:520 INFO  LoginPagePF :29 - Clicking Login button on Login screen
UserName verified
2021-05-28 08:05:690 INFO  HomepagePF :30 - Verifying user text
2021-05-28 08:05:148 INFO  HomepagePF :44 - Clicking Logout Div
2021-05-28 08:05:392 INFO  HomepagePF :46 - Clicking Logout Span
In teardown
```

Figure 11.5: Graceful logout for positive scenario

The negative scenario of verifying the Account Type is executed next which has an Assertion failure as follows:

```
2021-05-28 08:05:288 INFO  LandingPagePF :26 - Clicking Login button on Landing page
UserName is: chaubalpinakin@gmail.com
2021-05-28 08:05:145 INFO  LoginPagePF :21 - Entering username
Password is: Pc9121975!
2021-05-28 08:05:287 INFO  LoginPagePF :25 - Entering password
Login button clicked
2021-05-28 08:05:458 INFO  LoginPagePF :29 - Clicking Login button on Login screen
Account type verified
2021-05-28 08:05:561 INFO  HomepagePF :37 - Verifying account type
In teardown
In teardown failure
```

Figure 11.6: Console log for negative scenario

The exact assertion failure is shown as follows:

```
[31mjava.lang.AssertionError: expected [Free account1] but found [Free account]
  at org.testng.Assert.fail(Assert.java:96)
  at org.testng.Assert.failNotEquals(Assert.java:776)
  at org.testng.Assert.assertEqualsImpl(Assert.java:137)
  at org.testng.Assert.assertEquals(Assert.java:118)
  at org.testng.Assert.assertEquals(Assert.java:453)
  at org.testng.Assert.assertEquals(Assert.java:463)
  at pageobjectspf.HomepagePF.verifyAccountType(HomepagePF.java:38)
  at stepdefinitions.HomePageStepDefPF.the_user_should_be_shown_for_the_account_type(HomePageStepDefPF.java:22)
  at ?.Then The user should be shown "Free account1" for the account type(HappyFlowFeaturePF.feature:20)
```

Figure 11.7: Assertion error for negative scenario

Now comes the exciting time to see the reports that got generated from this test run that we will look at in the next section.

11.8 Examining the Cucumber-JVM reports

After the test execution, it is time to take a look at the statistical and graphical reports generated from the test run. Navigate to the folder shown in the following screenshot in Eclipse:

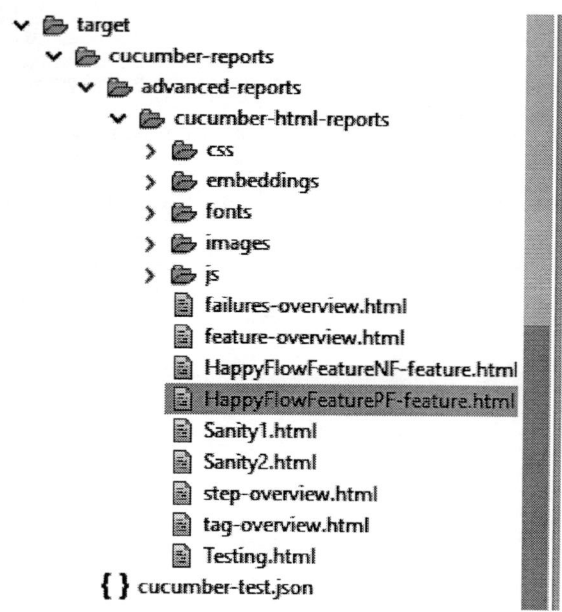

Figure 11.8: Generated reports

We will take to take a look at the three reports **`HappyFlowFeaturePF-feature.html`**, **`HappyFlowFeatureNF-feature.html`**, and **`Sanity1.html`**.

11.8.1 Examining the HappyFlowFeaturePF-feature.html

This report has details about the positive and negative scenarios from the **`HappyFlowFeaturePF.feature`** feature file. The report shows one passed and one failed scenario:

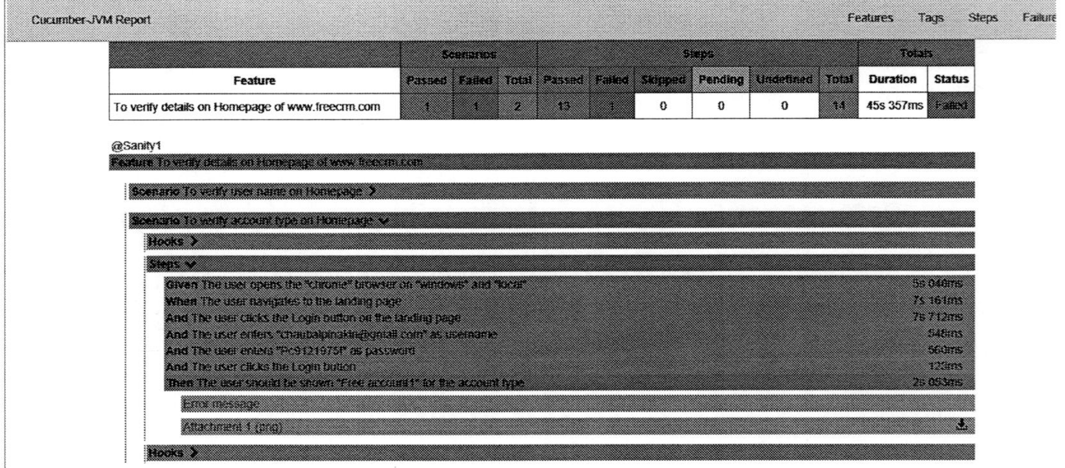

Figure 11.9: *Report output for positive and negative scenarios*

The failed scenario has a screenshot attached as shown in the following screenshot:

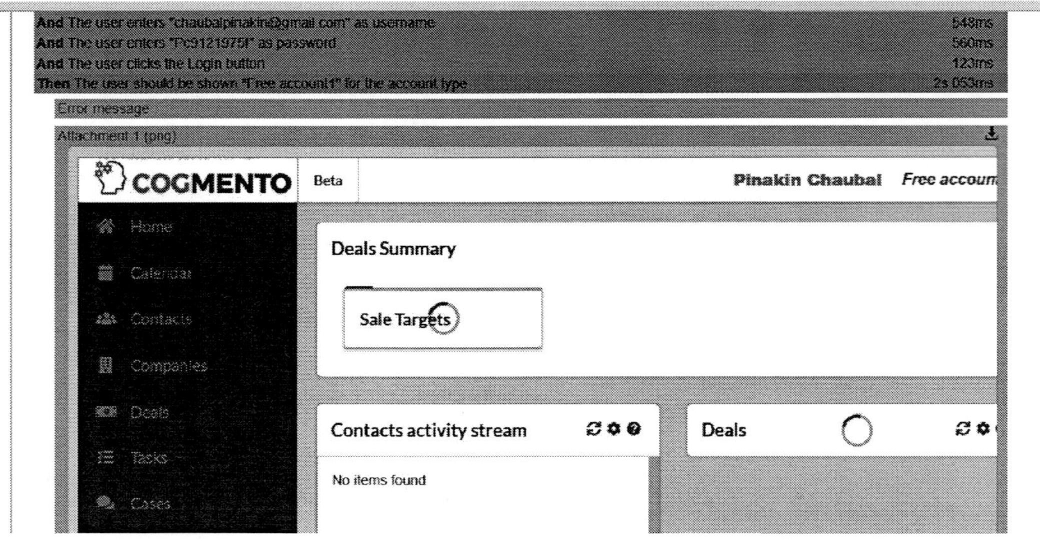

Figure 11.10: *Screenshot captured for negative scenarios*

Let's take a look at **`HappyFlowFeatureNF-feature.html`**.

11.8.2 Examining the HappyFlowFeatureNF-feature.html

This report has details about one negative scenario from the **`HappyFlowFeatureNF.feature`** feature file. The report is displayed in the following screenshot:

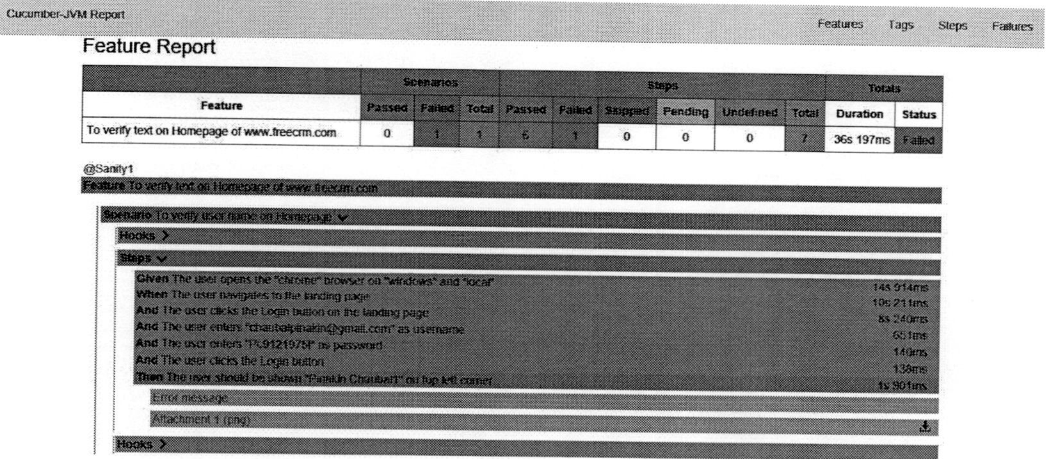

Figure 11.11: Report for Negative scenarios

The step that failed has a screenshot attached as shown in the following screenshot:

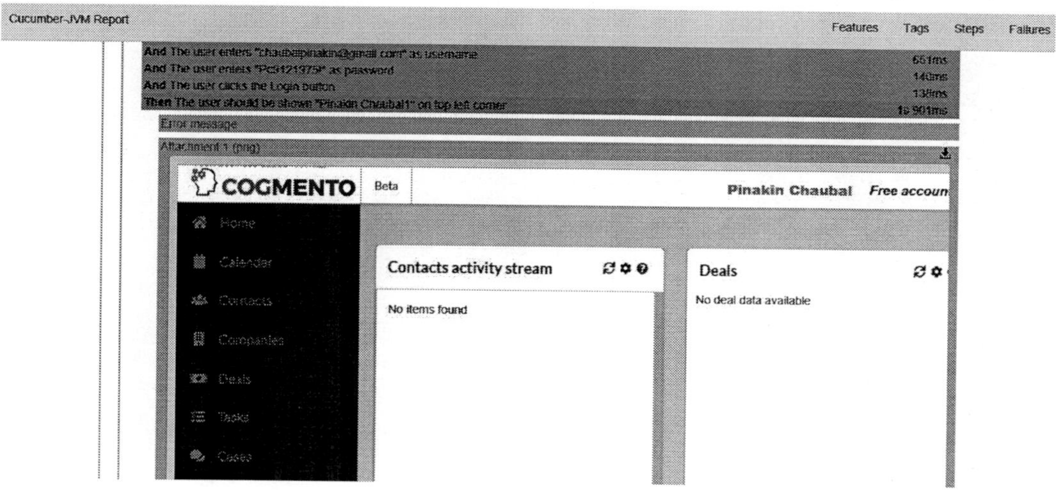

Figure 11.12: Screenshot for Negative scenarios

Next, we will take a look at the report based on the tag **`@Sanity1`**.

11.8.3 Examining the Sanity1.html

This is a consolidated report which contains data from **`HappyFlowFeaturePF.feature`**, **`HappyFlowFeatureNF.feature`** feature files as shown in the following screenshot. We have two failures and one pass. We have two screenshots and two error messages.

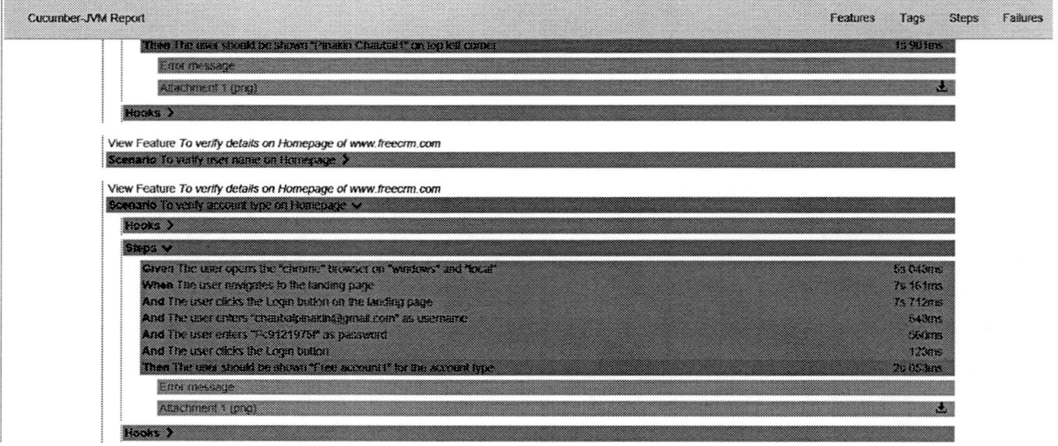

Figure 11.13: Screenshot for execution based on Tag

The error message in a failed scenario is displayed in the following screenshot:

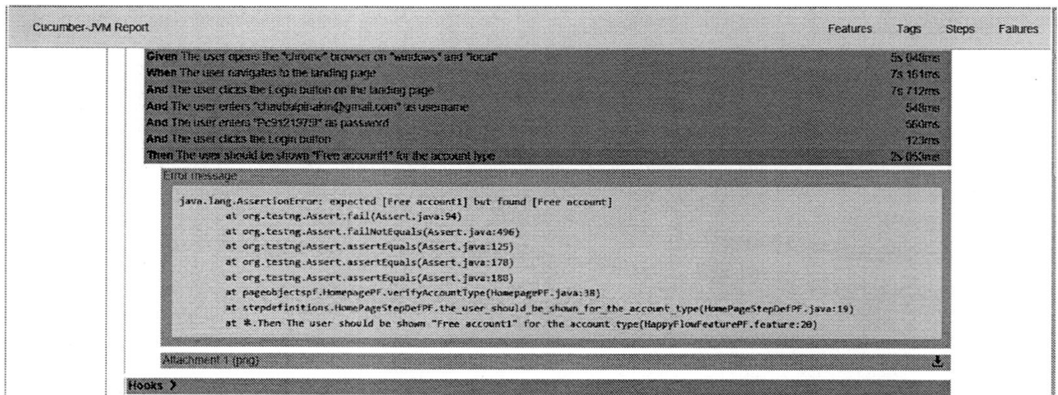

Figure 11.14: Screenshot for an error message for a failed scenario

The **`Sanity1.html`** thus gives excellent information on the passes and failures.

11.8.4 Examining the feature-overview.html

This is the complete summary of the execution along with the pass/fail percentages.

We also get beautiful pie charts in the report as shown in the following screenshot:

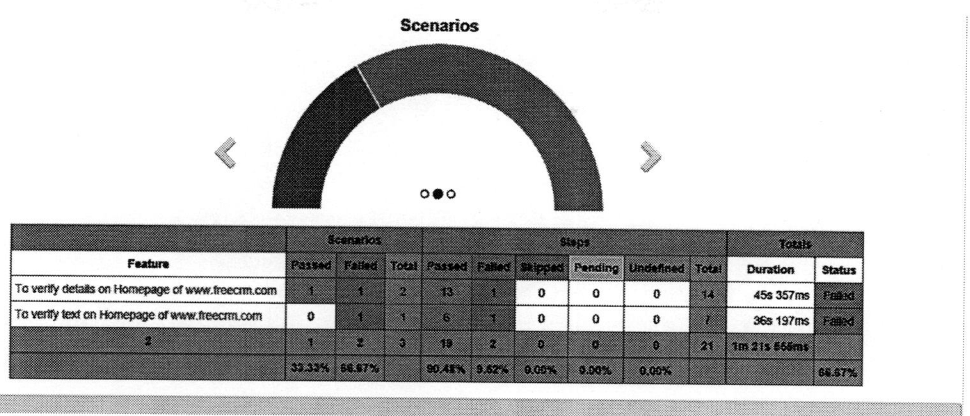

	Scenarios			Steps						Totals	
Feature	Passed	Failed	Total	Passed	Failed	Skipped	Pending	Undefined	Total	Duration	Status
To verify details on Homepage of www.freecrm.com	1	1	2	13	1	0	0	0	14	45s 357ms	Failed
To verify text on Homepage of www.freecrm.com	0	1	1	6	1	0	0	0	7	36s 197ms	Failed
2	1	2	3	19	2	0	0	0	21	1m 21s 555ms	
	33.33%	66.67%		90.48%	9.52%	0.00%	0.00%	0.00%			66.67%

***Figure 11.15**: Consolidated report with a pie chart showing execution based on tags*

We have gone through the procedure of configuring the Cucumber-JVM reports and generated these reports by running a test suite with the **`@Sanity1`** tag.

Conclusion

This chapter covered the configuration and generation of Cucumber-JVM reports. We started by explaining the **`<testFailureIgnore>`** tag through which we can ignore failures and move ahead without stopping the test execution. We took a look at the Maven-Cucumber-Reporting plugin. We looked at a very common utility code for capturing screenshots on failures. We modified our TestRunner to work with the Cucumber JVM reports. We created a feature file with two scenarios one positive and one negative. We created another feature file with one negative scenario. We made changes to the Homepage page object, step definition, and locator where we added a new locator for the Account Type and the required glue and Java code. We then executed both feature files by giving them a common tag of **`@Sanity1`**. Finally, we took a look at the beautiful JVM reports for the individual feature files and tags.

In the next chapter 'Chapter 12, *Reporting using Extent Reports*', we will take a look at configuring the extent reports which can be customized to our needs, and we can also put log statements and screenshots in the Extent reports. We will see the detailed process of using Extent reports in the framework.

Questions

1. Explain the <testFailureIgnore> tag in pom.xml.
2. List the sections in the Maven-Cucumber-Reporting plugin.
3. Modify your testrunner and try generating the JVM reports.
4. Create a method for capturing screenshots.
5. Execute the test suite with a combination of positive and negative scenarios using Maven.

CHAPTER 12
Reporting Using Extent Reports

In the previous chapter, we looked at the generation of the Cucumber JVM reports. We learned about the **`<testFailureIgnore>`** tag. We added a plugin called the *maven-cucumber-reporting* plugin which we used for generating beautiful HTML reports. We created one positive scenario and one negative scenario in the first feature file and one negative scenario in the second feature file and placed the same tag on both the feature files. We modified the test runner class to generate Cucumber JVM reports. The scenarios got executed in a serial fashion generating a report for each feature file and a consolidated report based on tags.

In this chapter, we will learn the configuration required for generating Extent reports. Extent reports are another set of reports that help us in understanding the status of execution through graphical representations. These reports are customizable reports where the reports can be customized on basis of our needs. We will create a new class for generating Extent reports. This class will generate one report for all feature files. We will attach a screenshot in the report for failed scenarios.

Structure

The following topics will be covered in this chapter:

- Introduction to Extent reports
- Understanding Maven dependency for Extent reports

- Creating a class for generating Extent reports
- Creating a helper class for taking screenshots
- Creating a base steps class for declaring the required variables
- Understanding changes to the Before and After hooks
- Executing the flows and generating the reports

Objectives

After reading this chapter, the reader will be able to:

- Understand what Extent reports are
- Understand Maven dependency for Extent reports
- Create a class for generating Extent reports
- Create a helper class for taking screenshots
- Create a base steps class for declaring required variables
- Understand changes to the Before and After Hooks
- Understand feature file execution and generate the reports

Let's start by understanding what Extent reports are along with the Maven dependency.

12.1 Introduction to Extent reports

Extent reports offer several features (when compared to the built-in reports that are generated through Cucumber). These reports include pie chart generation, scenario-wise report generation, adding screenshots, and so on, for every failed scenario and a beautiful user interface that can be shared with all stakeholders of the project.

12.1.1 Advantages of Extent reports

There are several advantages provided by extent reports and few of them are discussed as follows:

- HTML reports with pie chart representation, which is customizable
- Displays the time taken for scenario execution
- Multiple test case runs within a single suite can be tracked easily
- It can be integrated with TestNG and JUnit frameworks quite easily

12.1.2 Components of Extent reports

We will use two classes of Extents reports:

- **ExtentReports** class: This class is mainly used for starting reporters and building reports. There should be one `ExtentReports` instance for the entire JVM.
- **ExtentHtmlReporter** class: This class creates a rich standalone HTML file. It provides several configuration options via the `config()` method.

We will create a Custom Reporter class for generating Extent reports. There will be a generic helper for capturing screenshots.

Let's look at what dependencies are required for incorporating Extent reports.

12.2 Maven dependency for Extent reports

For using extent reports, the following dependency needs to be included in `pom.xml`:

```
<!-- https://mvnrepository.com/artifact/com.aventstack/extentreports -->
<dependency>
<groupId>com.aventstack</groupId>
<artifactId>extentreports</artifactId>
<version>4.0.9</version>
</dependency>
```

Save the POM xml. Right click on the project and select **`Maven | Update Project`**.

This download required Maven JARs.

12.3 Creating a class for generating Extent reports

We will create a class called '`CucumberCustomReporter.java`' to create our Extent reports. This class will have the methods shown as follows:

- **createCustomTest(Scenario, String)**: This method gets the scenario title and error message if the scenario has failed. It creates a test using the status of the scenario using the `getStatus()` method of the `Scenario` object. If the scenario has failed, it attaches a screenshot as well as prints the error message to the report.

The **createCustomTest(Scenario, String)** method is shown as follows:

```
      public void createCustomTest(Scenario scenario,String
screenshotFile)
throws IOException {
            if (scenario!=null) {
                  String testName = getScenarioTitle(scenario);
                  String errMessage = fetchErrorMsg(scenario);
                  switch(scenario.getStatus().toUpperCase()) {
                  case "PASSED":
                        extentReports.createTest(testName).
pass("passed");
                        break;
                  case "FAILED":
                        System.out.println("in failed");
extentReports.createTest(testName).fail(errMessage).a
ddScreenCaptureFromPath(screenshotFile);
                        break;
                  default:
                        extentReports.createTest(testName).
fail("skipped");
                  }
            }
      }
```

We have used the **fetchErrorMsg(Scenario)** to get the error message attached to the scenario, and we need access to the **stepResults ArrayList** as follows:

Figure 12.1: The private stepResults arrayList

The following step 7 of a feature file has failed. We need to extract the error message shown in the following screenshot:

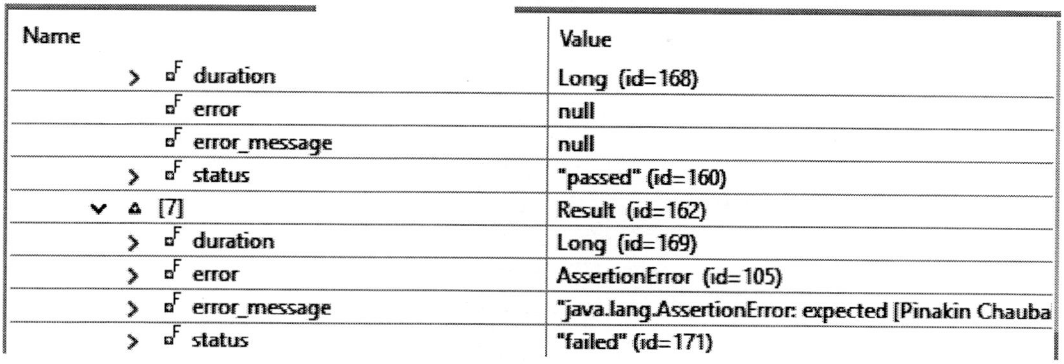

Name	Value
> duration	Long (id=168)
error	null
error_message	null
> status	"passed" (id=160)
∨ [7]	Result (id=162)
> duration	Long (id=169)
> error	AssertionError (id=105)
> error_message	"java.lang.AssertionError: expected [Pinakin Chauba
> status	"failed" (id=171)

Figure 12.2: The display of the error message

Here is the code for fetching the error message from the private **arraylist**. We declare two lists: one for the test result and one for the failed results. A field provides information about and dynamic access to a single field of a class or an interface. The reflected field may be a class (static) field or an instance field. Using this, we will fetch the **stepResults arraylist**. We then bypass the security on this field using the **setAccessible** method passing it the argument 'true'. We will fetch the step results for the scenario and store it into the local list **testResults**. We will then check for the test results being null or empty. If the test result list is not null or empty, we will use a lambda expression to extract the failed scenarios into the **failedResults** list. If the **failedResults** list is not null or empty, we will return the error message from this list. At the end, we will return spaces when the test has passed.

```
        private String fetchErrorMsg(Scenario scenario) {
                List<Result> testResults = null;
                List<Result> failedResults = null;
                try {
                        Field stepResults =
scenario.getClass().getDeclaredField("stepResults");
                        //Bypass the security
                        stepResults.setAccessible(true);
                        testResults = (List<Result>)stepResults.
get(scenario);
                } catch (NoSuchFieldException|SecurityException |
IllegalArgumentException | IllegalAccessException e) {
```

```
                // TODO Auto-generated catch block
                e.printStackTrace();
            }

            if (testResults != null && !testResults.isEmpty()) {
                //pick the results where error message is not
    null
                failedResults = testResults.stream().
    filter((a) -> {
                    return a.getErrorMessage() != null;
                }).collect(Collectors.toList());
            }

            if (failedResults != null && !failedResults.
    isEmpty()) {
                return failedResults.get(0).getErrorMessage();
            }
            return "";

        }
```

Let's take a look at the logic for capturing screenshots which we will attach to a failed scenario.

12.4 Creating a helper class for taking screenshots

We will now create a generic helper class which will be used for capturing screenshots. This generic helper has a method for taking screenshots which is **`takeScreenShot(String)`**. This method takes the screenshot and copies it to the location specified as an argument. It then returns the path. The method is shown as follows:

```
    public String takeScreenShot(String aPath) {
        File screenshot =
((TakesScreenshot)SingletonDriver.getInstance().getDrvr()).getScre
enshotAs(OutputType.FILE);
        try {
```

```
            FileUtils.copyFile(screenshot, new File(aPath));
        } catch (IOException e) {
            e.printStackTrace();
            return "";
        }
        return aPath;
    }
```

We have the path to the screenshot with us now. Let's invoke this method from the After Hook. In order to declare the object of the **CustomCucumberReporter** class, to create a Boolean variable to check whether the **CustomCucumberReporter** class has been instantiated and to instantiate the **GenericHelper** class, we will make use of the Base class for the Before and After Hooks so that these hooks can use these objects. Let's create this class.

12.5 Create a base steps class for declaring required variables

We will create a Base Class (**BaseSteps.java**) to achieve the goals mentioned as follows:

- Create an object of type **CucumberCustomReporter.**
- Declare a Boolean variable to check whether an instance of the **CustomCucumberReporter** class has been created.
- Create an object of the **GenericHelper** class.

  The **BaseSteps.java** is shown as follows:

```
package stepdefinitions;

import utils.CucumberCustomReporter;
import utils.GenericHelper;

public class BaseSteps {
        protected static CucumberCustomReporter
cucumberCustomReporter;
        protected static boolean isReportRunning;
        protected static GenericHelper genericHelper = new
GenericHelper();
}
```

We will make the Before and After hooks inherit the **BaseSteps** class. Let's take a look at changes to the Before and After hooks.

12.6 Changes to the Before and After Hooks

We will now make changes to the Before and After Hooks. We are required to change classes **BPBSD_00.java** and **BPBSD_99.java**.

Let's take a look at the changes to the Before Hook.

12.6.1 Changes to the Before Hook

The Before Hook will extend the BaseSteps as follows:

```
public class BPBSD_00 extends BaseSteps
```

This is a comparatively small piece of code where we simply verify whether the **CustomCucumberReport** has been instantiated. If it has not been instantiated, then the instantiation is done and the '**isReportRunning**' boolean variable is set to true.

```
    @Before
    public void setUp(Scenario scenario) {
          System.out.println("Before  any of the methods");
          if(!isReportRunning) {
                cucumberCustomReporter=new
CucumberCustomReporter("src/test/resources/TestReport.html");
                isReportRunning = true;
          }
    }
```

Once the Before Hook is executed, the scenario is executed and finally the After Hook is executed. Let's see what we are achieving in the After Hook.

12.6.2 Changes to the After Hook

The After Hook will run after a scenario is executed. The After Hook also extends the **BaseSteps** class and the tear down method has the code that creates the Extent report. We will make use of the **getProperty(String)** method of the **System** class to get the project home directory and then append the remaining path along with the image file name. We will then invoke the **takeScreenShot(Sting)** method from the **GenericHelper** class in case of the scenario failure. We will then create an Extent test with the screenshot. Finally, we will flush the report by invoking the **writeReport()** method:

```
        @After
        public void tearDown1(Scenario scenario) throws IOException {
                File screenPrint = null;
                String screenshotName =
System.getProperty("user.dir")+"\\src\\test\\resources\\
images\\"+scenario.getName().replaceAll(" ", "")+".jpeg";
                if (scenario.isFailed()){
                        genericHelper.takeScreenShot(screenshotName);
                        byte[] screenPrint1 =
((TakesScreenshot)SingletonDriver.getInstance().getDrvr()).
getScreenshotAs(OutputType.BYTES);
                        scenario.embed(screenPrint1, "image/png");
                        try {
                                if (!(SingletonDriver.getInstance().
getSessId()==null)) {
                                SingletonDriver.getInstance().getDrvr().
close();
                                SingletonDriver.getInstance().getDrvr().
quit();
                                }
                        } catch (Exception e) {
                                // TODO Auto-generated catch block
                                e.printStackTrace();
                        }

                } else {
                        try {
                                if (!(SingletonDriver.getInstance().
getSessId()==null)) {
                                SingletonDriver.getInstance().getDrvr().close();
                                SingletonDriver.getInstance().getDrvr().quit();
                                }
```

```
                } catch (Exception e) {
                        // TODO Auto-generated catch block
                        e.printStackTrace();
                }
        }
        cucumberCustomReporter.createCustomTest(scenario, screenshotName);
        cucumberCustomReporter.writeReport();
}
```

Finally, we come to the point where we will see Extent reports in action.

12.7 Execution of the flows and generating the reports

Right click on the **pom.xml** and click on **Run As | Maven Install**. The tests get executed and the logs get printed in the console as shown in the following screenshot. Please note that F*igure 12.3* is just a partial snapshot of the log.

```
@Sanity1
Feature: To verify details on Homepage of www.freecrm.com
Before  any of the methods
Sep 30, 2020 9:23:56 AM org.openqa.selenium.remote.DesiredCapabilities chrome
INFO: Using `new ChromeOptions()` is preferred to `DesiredCapabilities.chrome()`
Starting ChromeDriver 83.0.4103.39 (ccbf011cb2d2b19b506d844400483861342c20cd-refs/branch-heads/4103@{#416}) on port 13956
Only local connections are allowed.
Please see https://chromedriver.chromium.org/security-considerations for suggestions on keeping ChromeDriver safe.
ChromeDriver was started successfully.
Sep 30, 2020 9:24:00 AM org.openqa.selenium.remote.ProtocolHandshake createSession
INFO: Detected dialect: W3C

*** THE TEST ENVIRONMENT DETAILS ARE CHROME||WINDOWS||LOCAL||Selenium Version is3.141.59||Session ID=e4a31d9fb415ce1704f5a9c2ec1f650a

2020-09-30 09:09:978 INFO  LandingPagePF :26 - Clicking Login button on Landing page
UserName is: chaubalpinakin@gmail.com
2020-09-30 09:09:872 INFO  LoginPagePF :21 - Entering username
Password is: Pc9121975!
2020-09-30 09:09:204 INFO  LoginPagePF :25 - Entering password
Login button clicked
2020-09-30 09:09:455 INFO  LoginPagePF :29 - Clicking Login button on Login screen
UserName verified
2020-09-30 09:09:545 INFO  HomepagePF :30 - Verifying user text
2020-09-30 09:09:160 INFO  HomepagePF :44 - Clicking Logout Div
2020-09-30 09:09:261 INFO  HomepagePF :46 - Clicking Logout Span
After all methods
D:\pinakin.chaubal\workspace\cucumberpom\src\test\resources\images\ToverifyusernameonHomepage.jpeg
Status of scenario: passed
Status of screenshotfile: D:\pinakin.chaubal\workspace\cucumberpom\src\test\resources\images\ToverifyusernameonHomepage.jpeg
```

***Figure 12.3**: Execution log for passed scenario*

Our report is available at "**src/test/resources/TestReport.html**". The report is shown in the following screenshot. Three scenarios have run from two feature files where two failed and one passed. The one that passed does not have a screenshot attached. *Figure 12.4* is a failed test case where the screenshot is in the form of a link. Click on the link to open the image:

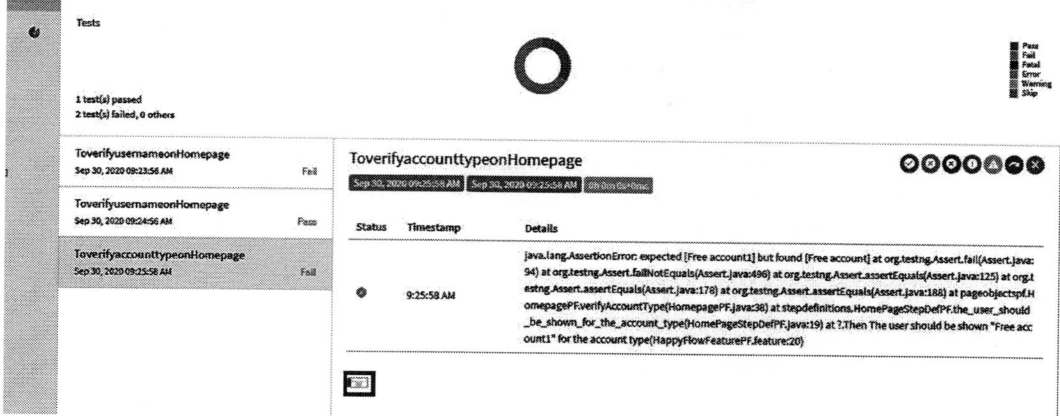

***Figure 12.4**: TestReport.html*

After clicking on the highlighted link, the following screen appears:

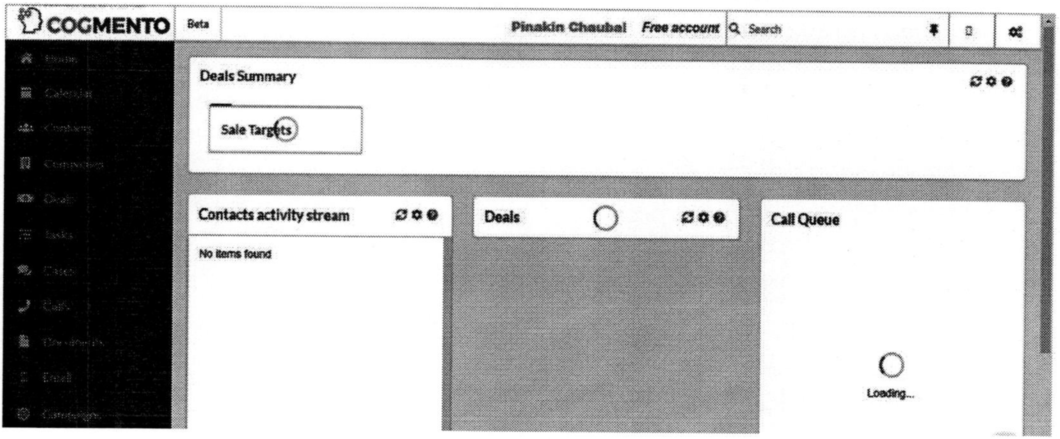

***Figure 12.5**: Snapshot.html*

We have configured Extent reports with our framework in this chapter. This brings us to the end of this chapter.

Conclusion

This chapter covered the configuration and generation of Extent reports. We got introduced to Extent reports. We understood what Maven dependency should be put in the **`pom.xml`** in order to generate Extent reports. We created a class for generating Extent reports. In addition to this, we created a generic helper class to take screenshots in case of scenario failures. We also used reflection in Java to extract the assertion error in case of failures. We printed this error in the Extent report. We went ahead and created a Base class for the Hooks for declaring required variables.

We made changes to Before and After hooks to generate Extent reports. Finally, we generated Extent reports for three scenarios.

In the next chapter '*Chapter 13, Parallel Execution Using Selenium Grid*', we will take a look at parallel execution in Cucumber using the **`ThreadLocal`** class. We will see changes required for **`POM.XML`** and **`TestNG.xml`** and we will also see changes. We will also see how we can generate Extent reports in parallel execution.

Questions

1. Explain the process of generating Extent reports.
2. Create a program to generate Extent reports for Cucumber scenarios.
3. Explain the concept of Reflection in Java.
4. Extract the Step Results private array list and try printing contents from it.
5. Explain how to attach screenshots in Extent reports.

CHAPTER 13
Parallel Execution Using Selenium Grid

In *Chapter 12, Reporting Using Extent Reports,* we learned how to create Extent reports version 4. We took a look at the Maven dependency for Extent reports. We created a custom class for generating the reports. We also added a generic helper class for taking screenshots. A base steps class for the hooks was created so that variables or objects common to both the classes could be declared here. We made changes to the before and after hooks. We executed the positive and negative flows and generated the Extent report.

This chapter will look at parallel execution on the local and Selenium Grid. Parallel test execution involves running test automation in parallel rather than sequentially. The tester need not execute your tests one by one. Instead of that, the entire batch can be split up into multiple groups, and each group can be executed in parallel. This technique has advantages that can effectively reduce the test execution time and improve your overall software development life cycle.

Once the reader completes reading this chapter, he/she will have sufficient knowledge to set up a test suite that will have tests that execute in parallel.

Structure

The following topics will be covered in this chapter:

- Introduction to parallel execution

- Understanding Synchronized methods
- Creating an Extent Manager class
- Creating an Extent Test class
- Changes to be made to the testng.xml for parallel execution
- Changes to the Step Definitions for logging
- Looking at the Singleton Driver code
- Improved versions of the Before and After Hooks
- Executing the pom.xml to generate the reports
- Introduction to Remote Web Driver
- Learning about the Selenium standalone server
- Introduction to Selenium Grid
- Changes to be made to the feature files and Test Runner
- Executing the test cases on the configured grid

Objectives

After reading this chapter, the reader will be able to:

- Understand parallel execution
- Understand synchronized methods
- Create an Extent Manager class
- Create an Extent Test class
- Change the **`testng.xml`** for parallel execution
- Make changes to the Step Definitions for logging purpose
- Understand the Singleton Driver code
- Understand improved Before and After Hooks
- Understand the execution of the **`pom.xml`** to generate the reports
- Introduce Remote Web Driver
- Learn about the Selenium standalone server
- Introduce Selenium Grid
- Make changes to the feature files and Test Runner
- Execute the test cases on the configured grid

Let's start understanding the concepts related to parallel execution along with the Selenium Grid configuration. This is going to be a very important chapter as far as test automation is concerned.

13.1 Understand parallel execution

Parallel execution helps to reduce the execution time by executing Feature files or scenarios in parallel. This helps in faster turnaround time in case of failures. We can mix and match the execution on different browsers and thus achieve multi browser testing. We can also execute the test cases remotely using Grid as we will see later.

If one has enough resources to run all the tests at once, then the duration of the test execution will last only as long as the slowest running test. For example, if you have 100 tests and 100 virtual machines on which to run these tests, then dividing these tests in parallel will allow running 100 tests at once. If your slowest test among the set of 100 takes two minutes to run, then that is how long it will take for the entire test suite to complete the execution.

Let's now understand synchronized methods.

13.2 Understanding Synchronized methods

Synchronization in Java gives the control to access multiple threads to any resource that is shared.

Java synchronization is a good option when it is required that only one thread should be able to access the shared resource. Synchronization is mostly used in programming when we want to prevent the thread interference.

There are two types of synchronization in Java:

- Process synchronization
- Thread synchronization

We will look at only Thread synchronization here. There are two types of synchronizations available in Thread synchronization:

- Inter thread communication
- Mutually Exclusive
    1. Synchronized method
    2. Synchronized block
    3. Static synchronization

Here, our focus will be on synchronized methods. Synchronized methods enable us to prevent thread interference and prevent memory consistency errors. If an object is visible to more than one thread, all reads or writes to that object's fields are done through the **synchronized** method.

When the method is static synchronized, the lock is obtained on the class and not on the object. In general, synchronized methods are used to protect access to resources that are accessed concurrently or in parallel. When a resource that is being accessed concurrently belongs to each instance of your class, you use a synchronized instance method; when the resource belongs to all instances (i.e. when it is in a static variable as our **ExtentTest** and **ExtentReports** objects as we will see later), then you will use a synchronized static method to access it.

We will use static synchronized methods for the creation of Extent reports. We will have two classes, namely, **ExtentMgr** and **ExtentTstClass**. Let's see what these classes will have.

13.3 Creating an Extent Manager class

Our first class the **ExtentMgr** will have two methods, namely, **getReporter()** and **captureScreenshot()**.

Let's understand the various details in the **ExtentMgr** class.

1. Declare various variables for **ExtentReports**, Date, File name, Screenshot path, and Screenshot name as follows:

```
static ExtentReports extentReports;
static Date d = new Date();
static String fileName = "Extent_" + d.toString().replace(":",
"_").replace(" ", "_") + ".html";
public static String screenshotPath;
public static String screenshotName;
static int counter=0;
```

2. The static synchronized method **getReporter()** returns the **ExtentReports** object **extentReports**. This method creates the **ExtentHtmlReporter** object by passing it the filename with the full path as argument. The theme, document title, encoding, and report name are set by invoking the **config()** method on the **ExtentHtmlReporter** object. A new **ExtentReports** object is then created and the **ExtentHtmlReporter** object is attached to it by invoking the **attachReporter(ExtentHtmlReporter)** method on the **ExtentReports** object. Various system information is set on the **ExtentReports** object by invoking the **setSystemInfo(String, String)**. The code is shown as follows:

```
    public synchronized static ExtentReports getRprtr() {
        if (extentReports == null) {
                ExtentHtmlReporter htmlReprtr = new
ExtentHtmlReporter(System.getProperty("user.dir")+"/reports
/"+fileName);
                htmlReprtr.config().setTheme(Theme.STANDARD);
                htmlReprtr.config().setDocumentTitle(fileName);
                htmlReprtr.config().setEncoding("utf-8");
                htmlReprtr.config().setReportName(fileName);
                extentReports = new ExtentReports();
                extentReports.attachReporter(htmlReprtr);
                extentReports.setSystemInfo("Automation Test Run",
"Parallel Execution");
                extentReports.setSystemInfo("Organization", "BPB");
                extentReports.setSystemInfo("Build no", "BPB-TEST");
        }
        return extentReports;
    }
```

3. Create a method for capturing screenshots. This method will capture a screenshot as a file object. It creates the screenshot name by appending today's date and a counter that gets incremented on every call to this method. Finally, the screenshot is copied to the reports folder as follows:

```
    public static void captureScreenshot() {
            counter = counter + 1;
            File scrFile = ((TakesScreenshot)
SingletonDriver.getInstance().getDrvr()).
getScreenshotAs(OutputTyp e.FILE);
            Date d = new Date();
            screenshotName = d.toString().replace(":", "_").
replace(" ", "_")
+ "_"+counter+".jpg";
            try {
                    FileUtils.copyFile(scrFile, new
```

```
File(System.getProperty("user.dir") + "/reports/" +
screenshotName));
                } catch (IOException e) {
                        // TODO Auto-generated catch block
                        e.printStackTrace();
                }

        }
```

We will now move to the actual creation of logging statements inside the report using the **ExtentTstClass.java**.

13.4 Creating an Extent Test class

Follow the given steps to create the **ExtentTstClass.java**:

1. We will first create a **ThreadLocal** variable for **ExtentTest** and another variable for **ExtentReports** and fetch the **ExtentReports** instance using the **getRprtr()** method. Both these are static variables as follows:

```
public static ThreadLocal<ExtentTest> tstReprt = new
ThreadLocal<ExtentTest>();

static ExtentReports extent = ExtentMgr.getRprtr();
```

2. Fetch the test using the static synchronized method as follows:

```
        public static synchronized ExtentTest getTest() {


                return tstReprt.get();
        }
```

3. Create log messages for info, passed steps, and failed steps as follows:

```
public static void logInfo(String message) {

        tstReprt.get().info(message);
}

public static void logPass(String message) {

        tstReprt.get().pass(message);
}

public static void logFail(String message) {
```

```
        tstReprt.get().fail(message);
    }
```

4. Create a static method for marking the test case as passed using **`createLabel(String,ExtentColor)`** of the **`MarkupHelper`** class. Pass the log message and the GREEN enum entry. Get the **`ThreadLocal`** variable and pass it the status PASS along with the log message as follows:

```
public static void scenarioPass() {

        String passMsg = "Scenario has passed";

        Markup m = MarkupHelper.createLabel(passMsg, ExtentColor.
GREEN);

        tstReprt.get().log(Status.PASS, m);
}
```

5. Create a static synchronized method for adding screenshots in case of failure in which first invoke the **`captureScreenshot()`** static method from the **`ExtentMgr`** class. Put a fail log and attach a screenshot using the **`MediaEntityBuilder`**. Create a label using the **`createLabel(String,ExtentColor)`** of the **`MarkupHelper`** class. Pass the log message and the RED enum entry. Get the **`ThreadLocal`** variable and pass it the status FAIL along with the log message as follows:

```
public static synchronized boolean addScreenShotsOnFailure() {

                ExtentMgr.captureScreenshot();
                try {

                        tstReprt.get().fail("<b>" + "<font color=" +
"red>" +
"Screenshot of failure" + "</font>" + "</b>",

MediaEntityBuilder.createScreenCaptureFromPath(ExtentMgr.sc
reenshotName).build());
                } catch (IOException e) {


                }

                String failureLog = "Scenario has failed";

                Markup m = MarkupHelper.createLabel(failureLog,
ExtentColor.RED);

                tstReprt.get().log(Status.FAIL, m);
```

```
            return true;
        }
```

6. Create a method to start the generation of Extent reports. There are two overloaded methods as follows:

```
        public static synchronized ExtentTest startTest(String
testName) {
            return startTest(testName, "");
        }

        public static synchronized ExtentTest startTest(String
testName, String
desc) {
            ExtentTest tst = extent.createTest(testName, desc);
            tstReprt.set(tst);
            return tst;
        }
```

This completes the **ExtentTstClass**. Let's move on to changes in **testng.xml** for parallel execution.

13.5 Changes to the testng.xml for parallel execution

The changes to the **testng.xml** are simple. We have two tests. One is a positive test and the other is a negative test. In the suite tag, we have mentioned parallel="tests" so that the tests execute in parallel. We will execute two test runners here. The execution takes place based on the tags in both the test runners:

```
<?xml version="1.0" encoding="UTF-8"?>
<!DOCTYPE suite SYSTEM "http://testng.org/testng-1.0.dtd">
<suite name="Suite" parallel="tests">

  <test name="Negative Test">
    <classes>
      <class name="testrunner.BPBTR_2"/>
    </classes>
  </test> <!-- Test -->
```

```
        <test name="Positive Test">
    <classes>
      <class name="testrunner.BPBTR_3"/>
    </classes>
  </test>  <!-- Test -->

</suite> <!-- Suite →
```

Note: There should be one test runner for each feature file. The sample Test Runner is shown as follows:

```
package testrunner;

import java.io.File;

import org.testng.annotations.BeforeClass;
import org.testng.annotations.Test;

import cucumber.api.CucumberOptions;
import cucumber.api.testng.AbstractTestNGCucumberTests;
import cucumber.api.testng.TestNGCucumberRunner;

//import io.cucumber.testng.AbstractTestNGCucumberTests;
//import io.cucumber.testng.CucumberOptions;

@SuppressWarnings("deprecation")
@CucumberOptions(features = { "src/test/resources/featurefiles" }, glue =
{ "stepdefinitions" }, plugin = {
                    "pretty", "json:target/cucumber-reports/cucumber-
test.json" },tags= {"@PositiveSanity"})

public class BPBTR_2 extends AbstractTestNGCucumberTests {

}
```

Remember to change the tags on the feature files before executing the tests. Next, we move on to the changes made to the three Step Definitions in order to log statements in the extent reports.

13.6 Changes to the Step Definitions for logging

We will log info statements in the Extent reports by adding the piece of code shown as follows:

```
ExtentTstClass.logInfo("Verifying user text");
```

We will utilize the **logInfo(String)** method of the **ExtentTstClass** to log these info messages to the Extent report.

These statements should be introduced wherever applicable in all the three step definitions.

Now, we will take a look at the SingletonDriver code that helps us in executing feature files in parallel.

13.7 Looking at the SingletonDriver code

In the SingletonDriver, we have variables of type **ThreadLocal** defined as follows:

```
private ThreadLocal<WebDriver> webDriver =
    new ThreadLocal<WebDriver>();
private ThreadLocal<String> sessId =
    new ThreadLocal<String>();
private ThreadLocal<String> sBrwsr =
    new ThreadLocal<String>();
private ThreadLocal<String> sPltfrm =
    new ThreadLocal<String>();
private ThreadLocal<String> sVrsn =
    new ThreadLocal<String>();
```

Apart from these variables, we have setters and getters. The setter method creates a browser session that is Thread Safe. The SingletonDriver has been explained in detail in *Chapter 4, Learning about the TestRunner*. The signature of the method for setting the WebDriver is shown as follows:

```
public final void setDrvr(String, String, String, Map<String, Object>...)
```

The signature of the getter, which fetches the WebDriver instance is shown as follows:

```
public WebDriver getDrvr()
```

There are similar getters for session ID, Browser, Platform, and Version.

One common code that needs to be added after the switch block for browser is given as follows:

```
if ( envrnmnt.equalsIgnoreCase("grid") ) {
   webDriver.set(new RemoteWebDriver(new URL(remoteHubURL),caps));
}
```

We will now take a look at improved versions of the Before and After Hooks.

13.8 Improved versions of the Before and After Hooks

We have the improved versions of the setup and tear down methods. Let's see the improved version of the **SetupClass.java** which contains the **Before** hook. Here, we will set the scenario and start the **ExtentTest** in the **setUp(Scenario)** method as follows:

```
package stepdefinitions;

import com.aventstack.extentreports.Status;

import cucumber.api.Scenario;
import cucumber.api.java.Before;
import utils.ExtentMgr;
import utils.ExtentTstClass;

public class SetupClass {

        Scenario scenario;
        static String scenarioNm;
        @Before
        public void setUp(Scenario scenario) {
                this.scenario = scenario;
                scenarioNm = scenario.getName();
                ExtentTstClass.startTest(scenarioNm);
                System.out.println("Scenario started: "+scenario.getName());
                ExtentTstClass.getTest().log(Status.INFO, "Scenario started:
"+scenario.getName());
```

```
        }

}
```

Next, let's see the improved version of the **TearDown.java** which contains the **After** hook. Here, we will check the scenario object and if the scenario has failed, the log a failure message and add a screen shot by invoking the **addScreenShotsOnFailure()** static method of the **ExtentTstClass**. If the scenario has passed, log a pass message. Following this, if the session ID is not null, close and quit the driver, eventually by flushing the Extent report using the **flush()** method as follows:

```
        @After

        public void tearDown(Scenario scenario) {

        if (scenario.isFailed()) {

                        byte[] screenPrint =

((TakesScreenshot)SingletonDriver.getInstance().getDrvr()).
getScreenshotAs(OutputType.BYTES);

                        scenario.embed(screenPrint, "image/png");

                        ExtentTstClass.logFail("Scenario has failed");

                        ExtentTstClass.addScreenShotsOnFailure();

} else {

                        ExtentTstClass.logPass("Scenario has passed");

}

try {

                        if (!(SingletonDriver.getInstance().
getSessId()==null)) {

                                SingletonDriver.getInstance().getDrvr().close();

                                SingletonDriver.getInstance().getDrvr().quit();

                        }

} catch (Exception e) {

        e.printStackTrace();

}

ExtentMgr.getRprtr().flush();

}
```

Now, it is time to run the feature files parallelly. Let's trigger the run using the **`pom.xml`**. We have two feature files. One feature file (**`HappyFlowFeaturePF.feature`**) contains a positive scenario and a negative scenario and the other feature file (**`HappyFlowFeatureNF.feature`**) contains a negative scenario. What we will notice with this run is that firstly, two browser sessions will open and run one each scenario from each feature file. Later on, another browser session will open and execute the remaining scenario from the **`HappyFlowFeaturePF.feature`** feature file

13.9 Executing the test to generate the reports

Let's trigger the execution by right clicking on the pom and clicking on **`Run As | Maven Install`**. The log shown in the following screenshot gets printed where we will see two browsers opening at the same time. The printed logs indicate parallel execution in action.

```
ChromeDriver was started successfully.
ChromeDriver was started successfully.
Oct 04, 2020 7:59:52 AM org.openqa.selenium.remote.ProtocolHandshake createSession
INFO: Detected dialect: W3C

*** THE TEST ENVIRONMENT DETAILS ARE CHROME||WINDOWS||LOCAL||Selenium Version is3.141.59||Session ID=5cc48045afaa175b6cbc37d7725e50be

Oct 04, 2020 7:59:53 AM org.openqa.selenium.remote.ProtocolHandshake createSession
INFO: Detected dialect: W3C

*** THE TEST ENVIRONMENT DETAILS ARE CHROME||WINDOWS||LOCAL||Selenium Version is3.141.59||Session ID=9a999acdb15aa0fca830501e5618e94c

2020-10-04 08:10:321 INFO  LandingPagePF :26 - Clicking Login button on Landing page
2020-10-04 08:10:329 INFO  LandingPagePF :26 - Clicking Login button on Landing page
UserName is: chaubalpinakin@gmail.com
2020-10-04 08:10:121 INFO  LoginPagePF :21 - Entering username
Password is: Pc9121975!
2020-10-04 08:10:860 INFO  LoginPagePF :25 - Entering password
Login button clicked
2020-10-04 08:10:174 INFO  LoginPagePF :29 - Clicking Login button on Login screen
UserName is: chaubalpinakin@gmail.com
2020-10-04 08:10:420 INFO  LoginPagePF :21 - Entering username
UserName verified
2020-10-04 08:10:484 INFO  HomepagePF :30 - Verifying user text
Password is: Pc9121975!
2020-10-04 08:10:395 INFO  LoginPagePF :25 - Entering password
Login button clicked
2020-10-04 08:10:993 INFO  LoginPagePF :29 - Clicking Login button on Login screen
UserName verified
2020-10-04 08:10:101 INFO  HomepagePF :30 - Verifying user text
In teardown
In teardown failure
2020-10-04 08:10:340 INFO  HomepagePF :44 - Clicking Logout Div
```

***Figure 13.1**: Display of parallel execution*

The following screenshot shows how the Extent report looks like:

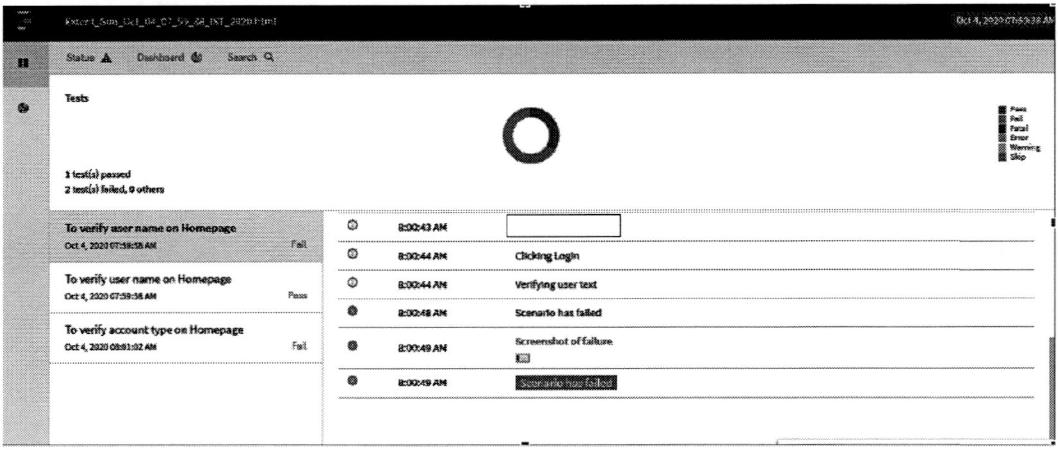

Figure 13.2: TestReport.html

Let's move on to understand what the Selenium Grid is and how we can execute remotely in parallel. We start with the introduction to RemoteWebDriver.

13.10 Introduction to Remote Web Driver

Until now, we have created our test scripts and executed them on browsers. All of these tests were executed against the browsers that were installed on a local desktop or laptop, where the test scripts reside. This may not be feasible at all times. There are chances that you may be working on Mac or Linux but want to execute your tests on Chrome on a Windows machine. This is where RemoteWebDriver comes into the picture.

`RemoteWebDriver` is a class implementing the WebDriver interface that a test-script creator can use to execute test scripts via the Selenium Standalone server on a remote machine. **`RemoteWebDriver`** consists of a server and a client. The test script uses the WebDriver client libraries, appropriate driver executable, and the actual browser sitting on the same machine.

The test script is located on a local machine, while the browsers are installed on a remote machine. This is where **`RemoteWebDriver`** comes into the play. As mentioned earlier, there are two components linked with **`RemoteWebDriver`**: the server and the client.

Let's understand the Selenium standalone server.

13.11 Learning about the Selenium standalone server

The Selenium standalone server listens on a port for various requests from a RemoteWebDriver client. Once it receives the requests, it sends them to any of the appropriate drivers, as requested by the RemoteWebDriver client.

The Selenium standalone server can be downloaded from the web. Let's download *version 3.141.59* of it, as we are using WebDriver.

Version 3.141.59. This server JAR should be downloaded and placed at an appropriate location on the remote machine on which the browsers are located. Also, make sure the remote machine has Java runtime installed on it. For this book, we will use the same machine as the server and client.

Let's now understand what a Selenium Grid is.

13.12 Introduction to Selenium Grid

Let's try to understand why we need Selenium Grid by analyzing a scenario. Suppose you have a web application that needs to be tested on the following browser-machine:

Combinations:

- Google Chrome on Windows 10
- Internet Explorer on Windows 10
- Firefox on Windows 10

We can simply alter the test script we created in the previous chapter and point to the Selenium Standalone Server running on each of these combinations (that is, Windows 10 with Google Chrome, Internet Explorer, and Firefox), as shown in the following code:

For Windows 10 and Chrome:

```
DesiredCapabilities caps = new DesiredCapabilities();
caps.setBrowserName("chrome");
caps.setPlatform(Platform.WIN10);
try {
driver = new RemoteWebDriver(new
URL("http://localhost:4444/wd/hub"), caps);
} catch (MalformedURLException e) {
```

```
e.printStackTrace();
}
driver.get("http://www.freecrm.com");
}
```

For Windows 10 and Internet Explorer:

```
DesiredCapabilities caps = new DesiredCapabilities();
caps.setBrowserName("internet explorer");
caps.setPlatform(Platform.WIN10);
try {
driver = new RemoteWebDriver(new
URL("http://localhost:4444/wd/hub"), caps);
} catch (MalformedURLException e) {
e.printStackTrace();
}
driver.get("http://www.freecrm.com");
}
```

For Windows 10 and Firefox:

```
DesiredCapabilities caps = new DesiredCapabilities();
caps.setBrowserName("firefox");
caps.setPlatform(Platform.WIN10);
try {
driver = new RemoteWebDriver(new
URL("http://localhost:4444/wd/hub"), caps);
} catch (MalformedURLException e) {
e.printStackTrace();
}
driver.get("http://www.freecrm.com");
}
```

In the preceding code, test scripts are tightly coupled to the machines that host the target platform and the target browsers. If the Windows 10 host changes, you need to alter your test script to handle that. This is not an optimized way to design your tests. The test scripts should focus on the functionality of the web application and not on the infrastructure that is used to execute these tests. There should be a central touchpoint to manage all the different environments. To solve this, Selenium Grid is used.

The Selenium Grid provides a cross-browser testing environment with several different platforms (such as Windows, Mac, and Linux) to execute our tests. The Selenium Grid is managed from a central point known as the **hub**. The hub has the information of all the different testing platforms also known as **nodes**. Nodes are the machines that have the desired operating systems and browser versions and are connected to the hub. The hub identifies and assigns these nodes to execute tests whenever the test scripts request them, based on the capabilities requested by the test script.

The following diagram gives a high-level view of the Selenium Grid:

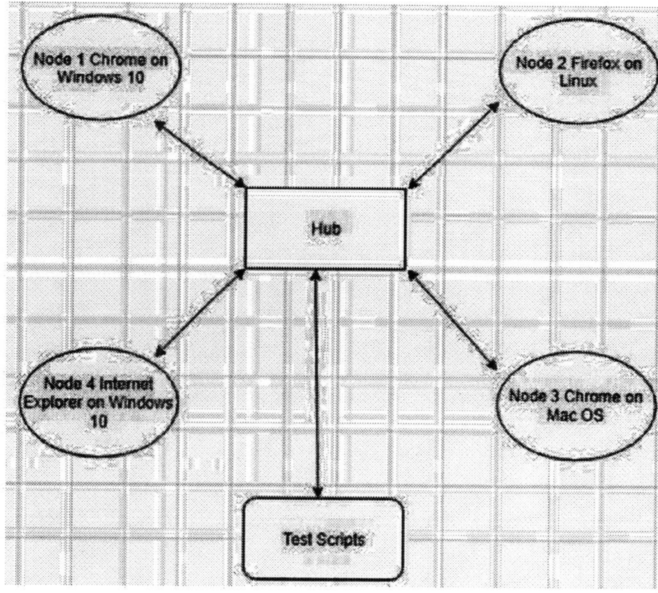

Figure 13.3: *Architecture of the Selenium Grid*

In the preceding diagram, there is one hub, four nodes of different platforms, and the machine where the test scripts are located. The test script will communicate with the hub and, in turn, request a target platform to be executed. The hub allocates a node with the desired target platform to the test script. The node executes the test script and sends the result back to the hub, which forwards the results to the test script.

Now that we have seen how the Selenium Grid works theoretically, let's learn the actual functioning of the Grid. We can use the same the Selenium Server standalone JAR file to be started in the hub mode on the hub machine, and a copy of the JAR file can be started in the node mode on the node machine. Let's start by understanding what the Hub is.

13.12.1 Introduction to the Hub

The hub is the center of a Selenium Grid. It maintains a registry of all the available nodes that are connected and part of a particular grid. The hub is nothing but a Selenium Standalone server running in the hub mode, listening on port 4444 of a machine by default. The test scripts will try to connect to the hub on this port. The hub re-routes the test-script traffic to the appropriate test-platform node. Let's see how to start a hub node. Navigate to the location of your Selenium server JAR file and execute the following command:

```
java -jar selenium-server-standalone-3.14.0.jar -role hub
```

Running this command will start your server in the hub mode. By default, the server starts listening on port 4444. You can start the server on the port of your choice. Suppose you want to start the server on port 2222; it can be done as follows:

```
java -jar selenium-server-standalone-3.14.0.jar -role hub -port 2222
```

The console output is shown in the following screenshot where the Grid hub has started on port 4444:

```
D:\pinakin.chaubal\workspace\cucumberpom>java -jar selenium-server-standalone-3.141.59.jar -role hub
11:14:19.308 INFO [GridLauncherV3.parse] - Selenium server version: 3.141.59, revision: e82be7d358
11:14:19.488 INFO [GridLauncherV3.lambda$buildLaunchers$5] - Launching Selenium Grid hub on port 4444
2020-10-04 11:14:19.972:INFO::main: Logging initialized @1360ms to org.seleniumhq.jetty9.util.log.StdErrLog
11:14:20.818 INFO [Hub.start] - Selenium Grid hub is up and running
11:14:20.816 INFO [Hub.start] - Nodes should register to http://192.168.0.20:4444/grid/register/
11:14:20.818 INFO [Hub.start] - Clients should connect to http://192.168.0.20:4444/wd/hub
```

Figure 13.4: Starting the Hub

If a browser session is opened and the **http://192.168.0.20:4444/** is loaded, the following page is displayed:

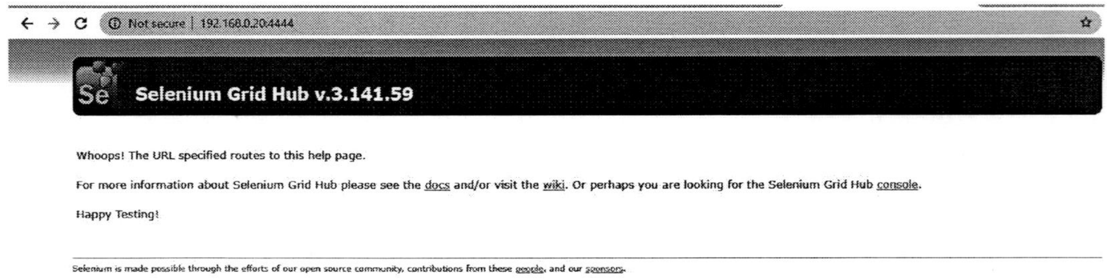

Figure 13.5: Console for the Hub

We don't have any nodes yet. Let's go ahead and launch our node. For launching the grid, we will require the driver executables. Download the driver executables from the Internet and place the executables in **`src/test/resources/executables`**.

13.12.2 Introduction to the Node

We have our hub is up and running. Let's start a node and connect it to our hub. Let's see how to start the node. The command to start the node and register with our hub is as follows:

```
java -Dwebdriver.chrome.driver=D:\pinakin.chaubal\workspace\cucumberpom\
src\test\resources\executables\chromedriver.exe -Dwebdriver.
ie.driver=D:\pinakin.chaubal\workspace\cucumberpom\src\test\resources\
executables\IEDriverServer.exe -Dwebdriver.firefox.driver=D:\pinakin.
chaubal\workspace\cucumberpom\src\test\resources\executables\
geckodriver.exe -jar selenium-server-standalone-3.141.59.jar -role node
-hub http://192.168.0.20:4444/grid/register -port 5555
```

Open a new command prompt and type the preceding command. The following screenshot displays the console. It shows that the node is registered with the hub and ready to use:

```
D:\pinakin.chaubal\workspace\cucumberpom>java -Dwebdriver.chrome.driver=D:\pinakin.chaubal\workspace\cucumberpom\src\tes
t\resources\executables\chromedriver.exe -Dwebdriver.ie.driver=D:\pinakin.chaubal\workspace\cucumberpom\src\test\resourc
es\executables\IEDriverServer.exe -Dwebdriver.firefox.driver=D:\pinakin.chaubal\workspace\cucumberpom\src\test\resources
\executables\geckodriver.exe -jar selenium-server-standalone-3.141.59.jar -role node -hub http://192.168.0.20:4444/grid/
register -port 5555
09:44:33.885 INFO [GridLauncherV3.parse] - Selenium server version: 3.141.59, revision: e82be7d358
09:44:34.010 INFO [GridLauncherV3.lambda$buildLaunchers$7] - Launching a Selenium Grid node on port 5555
2020-10-06 09:44:34.480:INFO::main: Logging initialized @1002ms to org.seleniumhq.jetty9.util.log.StdErrLog
09:44:34.705 INFO [WebDriverServlet.<init>] - Initialising WebDriverServlet
09:44:34.815 INFO [SeleniumServer.boot] - Selenium Server is up and running on port 5555
09:44:34.815 INFO [GridLauncherV3.lambda$buildLaunchers$7] - Selenium Grid node is up and ready to register to the hub
09:44:34.971 INFO [SelfRegisteringRemote$1.run] - Starting auto registration thread. Will try to register every 5000 ms.

09:44:35.612 INFO [SelfRegisteringRemote.registerToHub] - Registering the node to the hub: http://192.168.0.20:4444/grid
/register
09:44:36.240 INFO [SelfRegisteringRemote.registerToHub] - The node is registered to the hub and ready to use
09:45:29.892 INFO [ActiveSessionFactory.apply] - Capabilities are: {
```

Figure 13.6: Starting the Node

The console can be viewed as follows. The default configuration provides us with 5 Firefox, 5 Chrome, and 1 Internet Explorer instances as shown in the following screenshot:

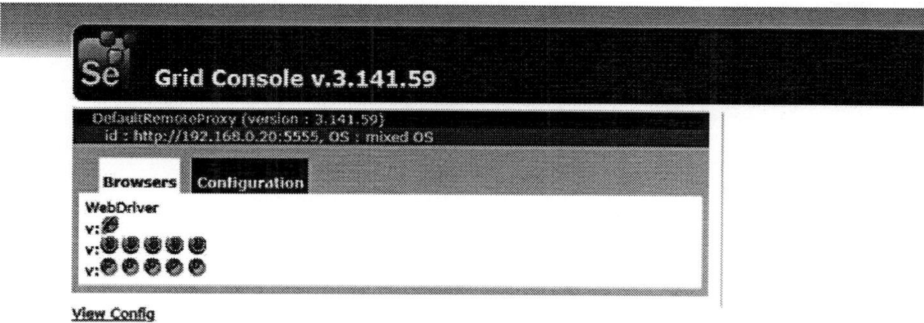

Figure 13.7: The Grid Console

Once the grid node is started and registered with the hub, the test can be triggered on the RemoteWebDriver.

13.13 Changes to the feature files and Test Runner

We will create two new feature files which are copies of **`HappyFlowFeaturePF.feature`** and **`HappyFlowFeatureNF.feature`**. Name these files **`HappyFlowFeaturePFGrid.feature`** and **`HappyFlowFeatureNFGrid.feature`**, respectively.

```
Given The user opens the "chrome" browser on "windows" and "grid"
```

Figure 13.8: Changes in the Feature file

We have replaced the word *"local"* with *"grid"*. Tag the **`HappyFlowFeaturePFGrid.feature`** with **`@PositiveGrid`** and **`HappyFlowFeatureNFGrid.feature`** with **`@NegativeGrid`**.

For the **`TestRunner`**, we need one Test Runner for each feature file. Create two Test Runners and mention tags as **`@PositiveGrid`** in one test runner and **`@NegativeGrid`** in the other test runner.

Now, we are all set to execute our feature files in parallel with the help of the grid.

13.14 Executing the test cases on the configured grid

Now that we have completed the configuration of the Selenium Grid, it's time to execute the feature files remotely. For this, right click on the **`pom.xml`** and click on **`Run As | Maven Install`**.

The logs are printed in the console as shown in the following screenshot:

```
*** THE TEST ENVIRONMENT DETAILS ARE CHROME||WINDOWS||GRID||Selenium Version is3.141.59||Session ID=d6d503f01b6ed3be7f8f3131f748eb13

Oct 04, 2020 5:07:57 PM org.openqa.selenium.remote.ProtocolHandshake createSession
INFO: Detected dialect: W3C

*** THE TEST ENVIRONMENT DETAILS ARE CHROME||WINDOWS||GRID||Selenium Version is3.141.59||Session ID=1282ee00be8624b4a90d47d7554d15f2

2020-10-04 17:10:258 INFO  LandingPagePF :26 - Clicking Login button on Landing page
2020-10-04 17:10:301 INFO  LandingPagePF :26 - Clicking Login button on Landing page
UserName is: chaubalpinakin@gmail.com
2020-10-04 17:10:439 INFO  LoginPagePF :21 - Entering username
Password is: Pc9121975!
2020-10-04 17:10:517 INFO  LoginPagePF :25 - Entering password
Login button clicked
2020-10-04 17:10:322 INFO  LoginPagePF :29 - Clicking Login button on Login screen
UserName is: chaubalpinakin@gmail.com
2020-10-04 17:10:812 INFO  LoginPagePF :21 - Entering username
UserName verified
2020-10-04 17:10:16 INFO  HomepagePF :30 - Verifying user text
Password is: Pc9121975!
2020-10-04 17:10:331 INFO  LoginPagePF :25 - Entering password
In teardown
In teardown failure
Login button clicked
2020-10-04 17:10:10 INFO  LoginPagePF :29 - Clicking Login button on Login screen
UserName verified
2020-10-04 17:10:349 INFO  HomepagePF :30 - Verifying user text
2020-10-04 17:10:736 INFO  HomepagePF :44 - Clicking Logout Div
2020-10-04 17:10:490 INFO  HomepagePF :46 - Clicking Logout Span
```

Figure 13.9: Creation of Logs

The tests get executed in parallel. The logger is thread safe by default and requires no changes for parallel execution. The logs appear in an interleaved fashion.

We will see some action in the open command prompt window for the node as shown in the following screenshot:

```
Only local connections are allowed.
Please see https://chromedriver.chromium.org/security-considerations for suggestions on keeping ChromeDriver safe.
Starting ChromeDriver 83.0.4103.39 (ccbf011cb2d2f19c506d844400483861342c20cd-refs/branch-heads/4103@{#416}) on port 3627
0
Only local connections are allowed.
Please see https://chromedriver.chromium.org/security-considerations for suggestions on keeping ChromeDriver safe.
ChromeDriver was started successfully.
ChromeDriver was started successfully.
17:03:01.458 INFO [ProtocolHandshake.createSession] - Detected dialect: W3C
17:03:01.600 INFO [ProtocolHandshake.createSession] - Detected dialect: W3C
17:03:01.616 INFO [RemoteSessionFactory.lambda$performHandshake$0] - Started new session 2cb1c5c3641e548ebe9a74acc23574
26 (org.openqa.selenium.chrome.ChromeDriverService)
17:03:01.633 INFO [RemoteSessionFactory.lambda$performHandshake$0] - Started new session 5205df8f83c2f16f1343bc2837e7a8
06 (org.openqa.selenium.chrome.ChromeDriverService)
17:04:18.853 INFO [ActiveSessions$1.onStop] - Removing session 5205df8f83c2f16f1343bc2837e7a806 (org.openqa.selenium.chr
ome.ChromeDriverService)
17:04:23.530 INFO [ActiveSessions$1.onStop] - Removing session 2cb1c5c3641e548ebe9a74acc2357426 (org.openqa.selenium.chr
ome.ChromeDriverService)
17:04:24.529 INFO [ActiveSessionFactory.apply] - Capabilities are: {
  "applicationCacheEnabled": false,
  "browserName": "chrome",
  "goog:chromeOptions": {
    "args": [
      "--disable-plugins",
```

Figure 13.10: Activity in the Selenium Grid Node console

The grid console shows two grayed out Chrome browsers which mean that two Chrome sessions are active as shown in the following screenshot:

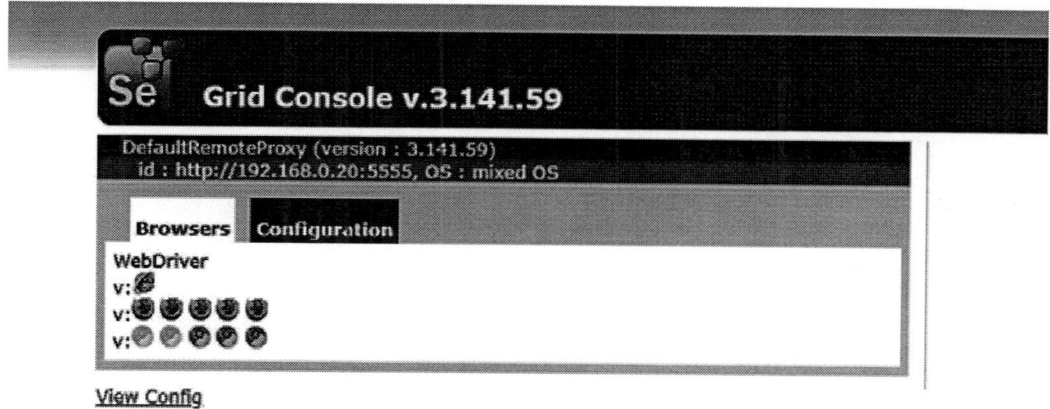

Figure 13.11: Browser instances in use

We thus come to the end of this chapter on parallel execution using the Selenium Grid.

Conclusion

This chapter covered parallel execution locally and on the Selenium Grid. We got introduced to parallel execution and synchronized methods. We created two classes for generating Extent reports to work with parallel execution in which we made use of Synchronized methods. We made changes to the **`TestNG.xml`** for parallel execution. In the suite tag, we simply added the parallel="tests" entry. We saw the changes required in the Step Definitions for creating logs in Extent reports. We did a recap on the configurations in the SingletonDriver for parallel execution and also introduced some code to launch browsers on the grid. We made changes to the Before and After hooks. We executed the **`pom.xml`** for parallel execution. We got introduced to the Remote WebDriver and Selenium Standalone Server. We learned about the Selenium Grid hub and node. We created two new feature files and test runners. Finally, we executed feature files in parallel on the grid.

In the next chapter 'Chapter 14, *Integration with Jenkins*', we will look at how we can integrate the framework with Jenkins. We will learn about Jenkins configuration and execute our feature Files using Jenkins. This will be an exciting chapter and the last chapter of our book as well.

Questions

1. Explain the advantages of parallel execution.
2. Give an example of a synchronized method.
3. Explain the changes to be made to the TestNG.xml for parallel execution.
4. Explain what a Selenium Grid is.
5. Create batch files to start the Selenium Grid Hub and Node.

CHAPTER 14
Integration with Jenkins

In the previous chapter, we looked at parallel execution. We understood what parallel execution is. We took a look at Synchronized methods and their usage. We created an Extent Manager class and Extent Test class to handle report generation in parallel execution. We made changes to the **`Suite`** tag of the TestNG xml to incorporate parallel execution. We introduced another Test Runner and executed it in parallel with the original Test Runner. We made changes to the Step Definition code, SingletonDriver code, and the Before and After hooks. We generated the Extent reports by executing the tests through **`POM.xml`**. We then looked at Remote WebDriver and Selenium Grid. We made the required changes to feature files and Test Runner.

In this chapter, we will learn how to integrate the framework with Jenkins. We will introduce you to Jenkins and download the Jenkins **`.war`** file. We will set up a Maven Project and configure Extent Reports. We will execute the test cases in parallel on the Grid and view the generated Extent reports on Jenkins. We will need to perform some prerequisites too which we will be going through.

Once the reader completes reading this chapter, he/she will have sufficient knowledge to set up a test suite to execute on the Grid in parallel.

Structure

The following topics will be covered in this chapter:

- Introduction to Jenkins
- Downloading the `jenkins.war` file
- Starting Jenkins
- Installing required plugins
- Creating the very first Maven job in Jenkins
- Executing the build from Jenkins
- Viewing the Extent reports in Jenkins

Objectives

After reading this chapter, the reader will be able to:

- Understand what Jenkins is
- Download the `jenkins.war` file
- How to start Jenkins
- Install required plugins
- Create the very first Maven job in Jenkins
- Execute the build from Jenkins
- View the Extent reports in Jenkins

Let's start understanding what Jenkins is. We will introduce Jenkins as an automation server that allows one to build, test, and deploy software. We will look at the build and test part in this chapter.

14.1 Introduction to Jenkins

Jenkins is an open-source Continuous Integration server that is capable of executing a chain of actions that help to achieve the Continuous Integration process through automation. Jenkins is free and written in Java. Jenkins is widely used for implementing continuous integration.

Jenkins can be run either standalone or along with a web server like Apache Tomcat. The reason Jenkins has become so popular is because of its monitoring of repeated tasks that come up during the development life cycle.

Jenkins helps to expedite the software development process, as Jenkins can automate build and test rapidly. Jenkins supports the complete software development life cycle from building, testing, documenting the software, deploying, and other stages of a software development lifecycle.

We start with downloading the `.war` file for Jenkins.

14.2 Download the jenkins.war file

The easiest way to get Jenkins on your system is to go to **http://jenkins.io**.

Click on the **`Download`** button as shown in the following screenshot:

Figure 14.1: Jenkins home page

Select the '**`Generic Java Package (.war)`**' option as shown in the following screenshot:

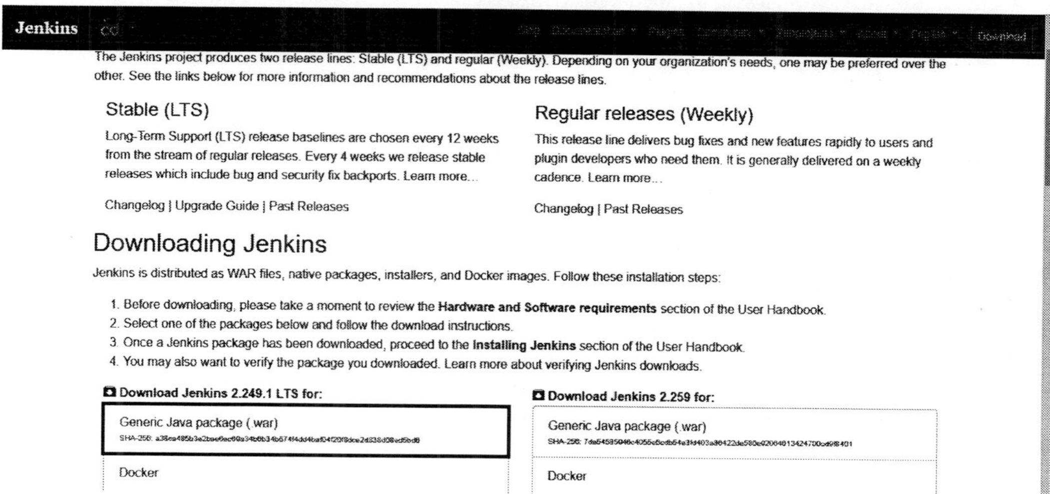

Figure 14.2: Jenkins war file

A file called `jenkins.war` gets downloaded to the system. Let's start Jenkins now.

14.3 Starting Jenkins

Starting Jenkins is pretty simple. Simply, open a command prompt, navigate to the folder where the **jenkins.war** file is located, and type the following command shown as follows:

```
java -jar jenkins.war
```

The logs start appearing in the console. Finally, when Jenkins is up, the message gets displayed in the console as shown in the following screenshot.

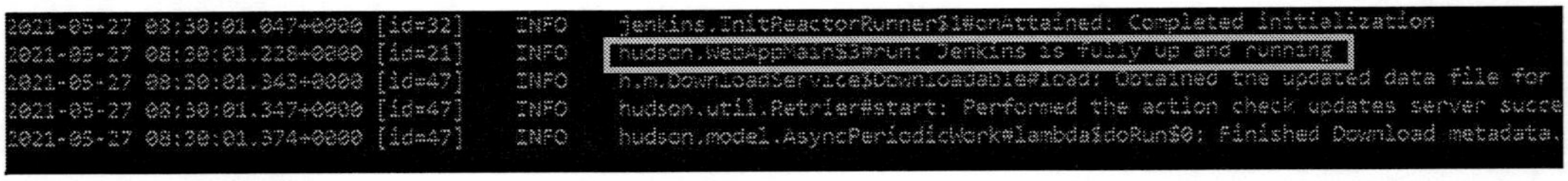

```
2021-05-27 08:30:01.047+0000 [id=32]    INFO    jenkins.InitReactorRunner$1#onAttained: Completed initialization
2021-05-27 08:30:01.228+0000 [id=21]    INFO    hudson.WebAppMain$3#run: Jenkins is fully up and running
2021-05-27 08:30:01.343+0000 [id=47]    INFO    h.m.DownloadService$Downloadable#load: Obtained the updated data file for
2021-05-27 08:30:01.347+0000 [id=47]    INFO    hudson.util.Retrier#start: Performed the action check updates server succe
2021-05-27 08:30:01.374+0000 [id=47]    INFO    hudson.model.AsyncPeriodicWork#lambda$doRun$0: Finished Download metadata.
```

Figure 14.3: Jenkins up and running

Open a browser and navigate to **http://localhost:8080**. The port for jenkins is 8080. The very first time an '*Administrator password*' gets generated and the path where this password exists is indicated. Navigate to the location, pick the password, and enter it on the screen where it asks for Administrator password. Click on **Continue**.

Select '**Install suggested plugins**' on the screen that appears. The default plugins get installed.

Create the first Admin user. Provide the username, password, and confirm the entered password, full name, and email address. Click on '**Save and Continue**'. On the next page, click on '**Save and Finish**'. On the next page, click on '**Start using Jenkins**'. The Jenkins home page is displayed.

14.4 Installing required plugins

We need to install plugins in order to use Jenkins with Maven and display Extent reports.

We will install the following two plugins:

- Maven integration plugin
- HTML publisher plugin

Let's start by understanding the Maven integration plugin.

14.4.1 Maven integration plugin

The Maven integration plugin helps us to build projects that use Apache Maven in Jenkins. Since ours is a Maven project, we will install the Maven integration plugin in Jenkins. Perform the following steps to install the Maven integration plugin:

1. Navigate to **http://localhost:8080** and select **`Manage Jenkins`** in the left panel.
2. Select '**`Manage Plugins`**' or '**`Go to plugin manager`**'.
3. Select the **`Available`** tab, and search for Maven Integration plugin.
4. Select the plugin and click on '**`Install without restart`**' or '**`Download now and install after restart`**' to install it.

As you install the plugin, other dependencies get installed as well.

After the installation, the plugin appears in the '**`Installed`**' tab as shown in the following screenshot:

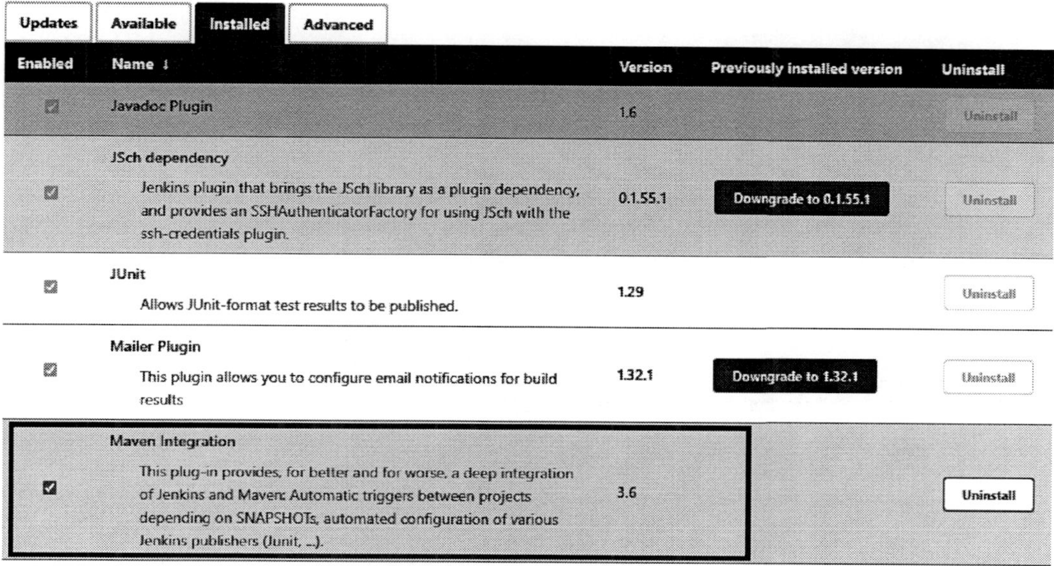

Figure 14.4: Maven Integration plugin

Let's next see the HTML publisher plugin.

14.4.2 HTML publisher plugin

The HTML publisher plugin is useful to publish HTML reports that your build generates to the job and build pages. It is designed to work with Maven and freestyle projects. It can also be used in a Jenkins pipeline. The HTML publisher plugin can be installed from the Jenkins installation connected to the Internet using the Plugin Manage screen. Once installed, the plugin can be configured as part of your Jenkins Maven/Freestyle job, or used in a Jenkins pipeline. The HTML publisher plugin can be configured in the post build portion of your Jenkins job.

Perform the following steps install the HTML publisher plugin:

- Navigate to **http://localhost:8080** and select `Manage Jenkins` in the left panel.
- Select '`Manage Plugins`' or '`Go to plugin manager`'.
- Select the `Available` tab, and search for HTML Publisher Plugin.
- Select the plugin and click on '`Install without restart`' or '`Download now and install after restart`' to install it.

After the installation, the plugin appears in the '`Installed`' tab as shown in the following screenshot:

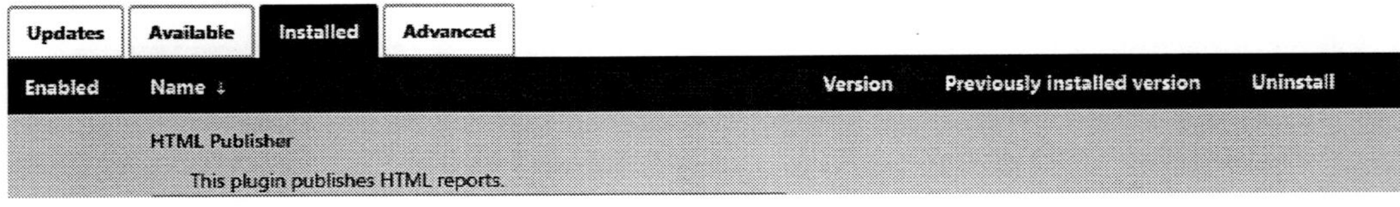

***Figure 14.5**: HTML Publisher plugin*

Now that we have installed the two required plugins, the Maven build and test job can be created in Jenkins.

14.5 Creating the very first Maven job in Jenkins

In order to create the Maven job in Jenkins, navigate to **http://localhost:8080** and click on the '`New Item`' menu in the left panel as shown in the following screenshot:

***Figure 14.6**: Creating a new job in Jenkins*

The next screen that appears is shown in the following screenshot. Enter an item name as '**`CucumberPOM`**' and select '**`Maven Project`**' as shown. Click on '**`OK`**'.

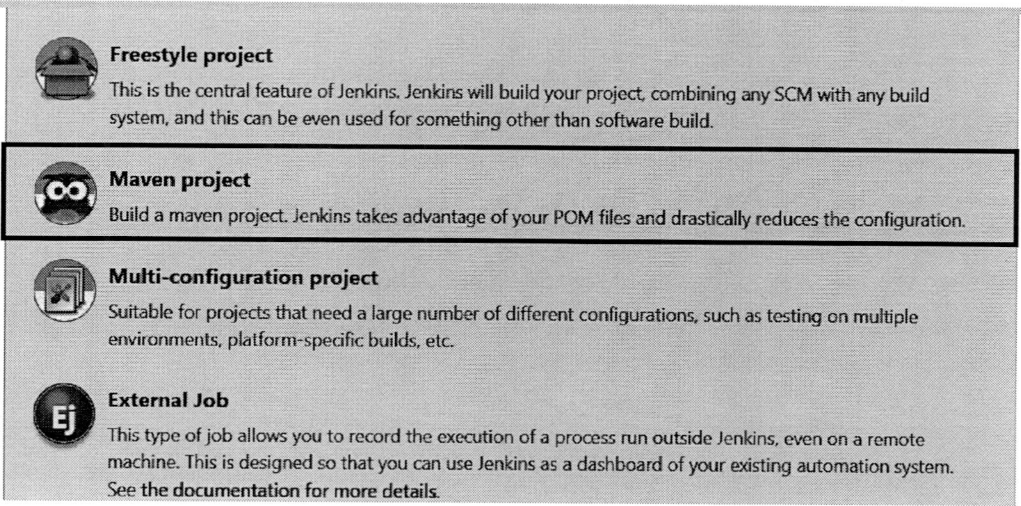

Figure 14.7: Selecting a Maven Project

On the next screen, click on the '**`Build`**' tab and enter the location of POM as '**`D:\pinakin.chaubal\workspace\cucumberpom\pom.xml`**' and '**`Goals and options`**' as install:

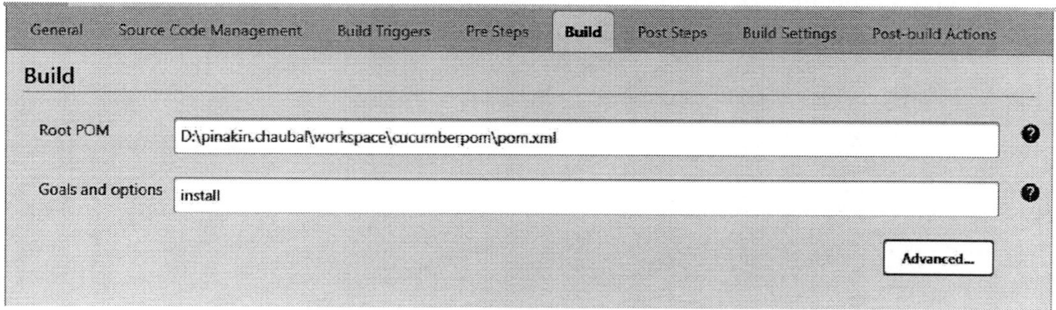

Figure 14.8: POM location and goals

Go to the Post-build **Actions** tab and click on **Add** post-build action | **Publish HTML reports** as shown in the following screenshot:

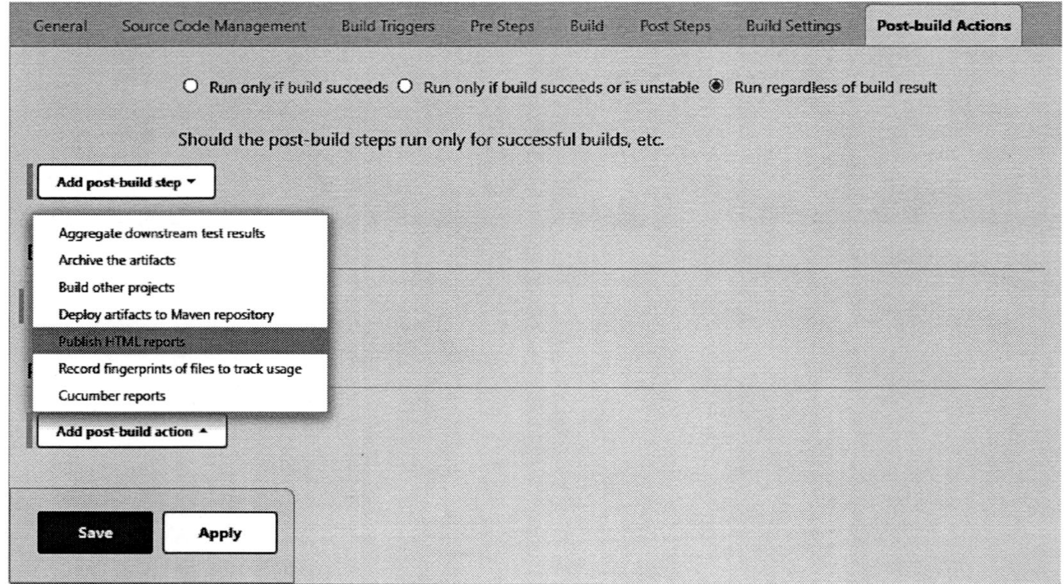

Figure 14.9: Selecting Publish HTML reports

Click on **Add** as shown in the following screenshot:

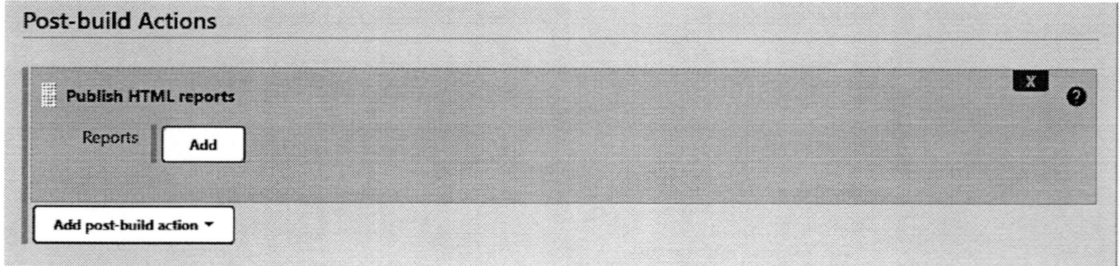

Figure 14.10: Configuring the report

Add the location of the reports in the field corresponding to '*HTML directory to archive*', and enter the '*Index pages*' as `*.html`. Enter the '**Report title**' as '**Extent Report**'. Click on '**Save**' as shown in the following screenshot:

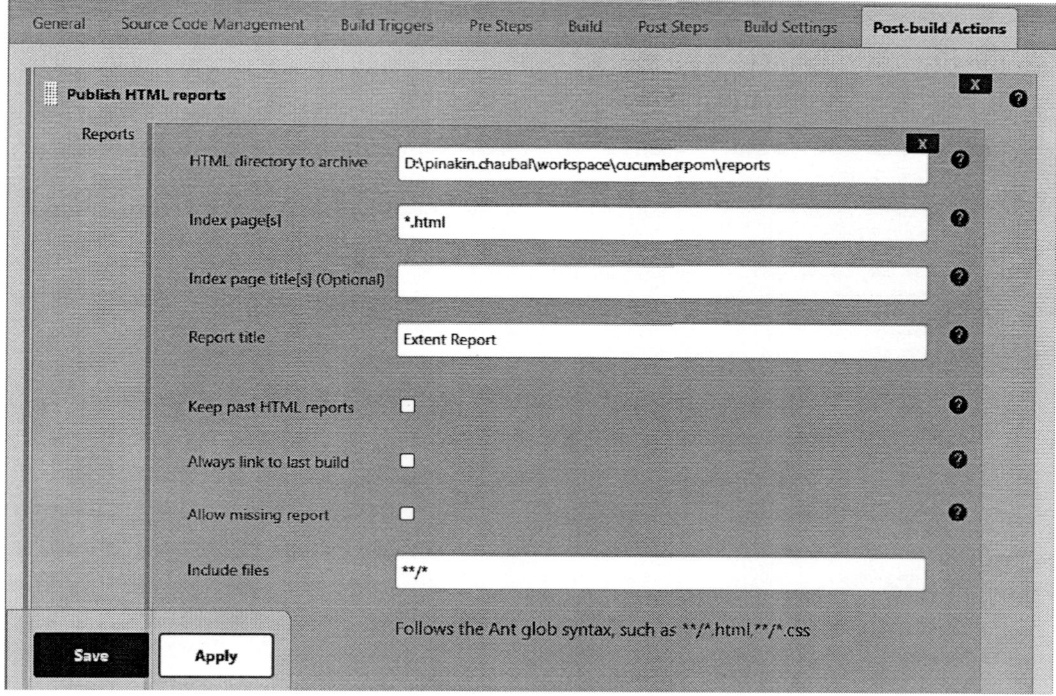

Figure 14.11: Specifying report details

That's all as far as the configuration is concerned. Let's now do the exciting part of executing the build from Jenkins.

14.6 Executing the build from Jenkins

We already have Jenkins running. Now, start the Hub and the Node. Click on Build now in the left panel as shown in the following screenshot:

Figure 14.12: Clicking on Build Now

After some time, logs start appearing and the parallel execution starts with two Chrome browsers opening. Tests get executed in parallel on the two browsers. The logs appear as shown in the following screenshot:

```
*** THE TEST ENVIRONMENT DETAILS ARE CHROME||WINDOWS||GRID||Selenium Version is3.141.59||Session ID=d717771013386cd09f1d1b182b9985dc


*** THE TEST ENVIRONMENT DETAILS ARE CHROME||WINDOWS||GRID||Selenium Version is3.141.59||Session ID=f737bfe88434abb5778ab4fc5ac614c4

2020-10-06 09:10:787 INFO  LandingPagePF :26 - Clicking Login button on Landing page
2020-10-06 09:10:42 INFO  LandingPagePF :26 - Clicking Login button on Landing page
UserName is: chaubalpinakin@gmail.com
2020-10-06 09:10:58 INFO  LoginPagePF :21 - Entering username
Password is: Pc9121975!
2020-10-06 09:10:866 INFO  LoginPagePF :25 - Entering password
Login button clicked
2020-10-06 09:10:806 INFO  LoginPagePF :29 - Clicking Login button on Login screen
UserName verified
2020-10-06 09:10:757 INFO  HomepagePF :30 - Verifying user text
In teardown
In teardown failure
UserName is: chaubalpinakin@gmail.com
2020-10-06 09:10:847 INFO  LoginPagePF :21 - Entering username
Password is: Pc9121975!
2020-10-06 09:10:67 INFO  LoginPagePF :25 - Entering password
Login button clicked
2020-10-06 09:10:685 INFO  LoginPagePF :29 - Clicking Login button on Login screen
UserName verified
2020-10-06 09:10:470 INFO  HomepagePF :30 - Verifying user text
```

Figure 14.13: Generation of logs

After the test execution, it is time to view the Extent reports.

14.7 Viewing the Extent reports in Jenkins

Click on the '**Extent Report**' link in the left panel as shown in the following screenshot:

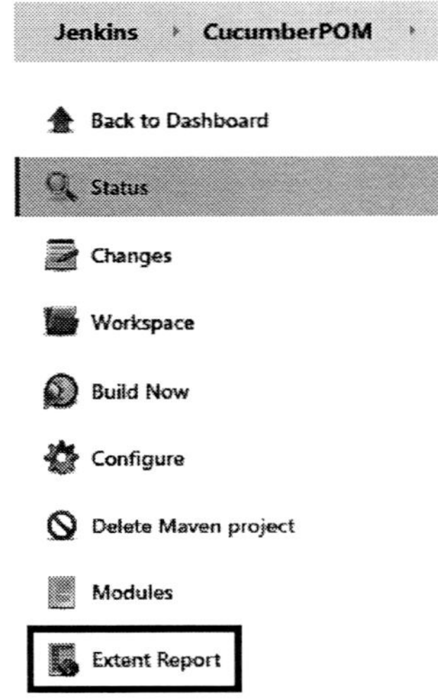

Figure 14.14: Viewing Extent Reports

The Extent Report location is opened in Jenkins as shown in the following screenshot:

Extent_Tue_Oct_06_09_45_27_IST_2020.html 06-Oct-2020 09:47:53 22.76 KB **view**

Figure 14.15: Generated Extent Reports

Click on the Extent Report and the report gets displayed in Jenkins as shown in the following screenshot:

1 test(s) passed
2 test(s) failed, **0** others

To verify user name on Homepage Oct 6, 2020 09:45:27 AM Pass	To verify user name on Homepage Oct 6, 2020 09:45:27 AM · Oct 6, 2020 09:46:57 AM · 0h 1m 29s+187ms
To verify user name on Homepage Oct 6, 2020 09:45:27 AM Fail	
To verify account type on Homepage Oct 6, 2020 09:47:02 AM Fail	

Status	Timestamp	Details
ⓘ	9:45:27 AM	Scenario started: To verify user name on Homepage
ⓘ	9:45:28 AM	Opening the browser: chrome

Figure 14.16: Extent Reports

In case a broken Extent Report gets displayed, go to the Console by clicking on '`Manage Jenkins`' on the Home page.

Scroll down and select '`Script Console`' as shown in the following screenshot:

Tools and Actions

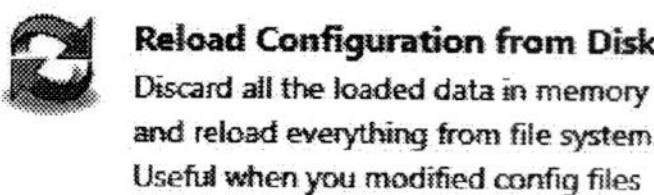

Reload Configuration from Disk
Discard all the loaded data in memory and reload everything from file system. Useful when you modified config files directly on disk.

Jenkins CLI
Access/manage Jenkins from your shell, or from your script.

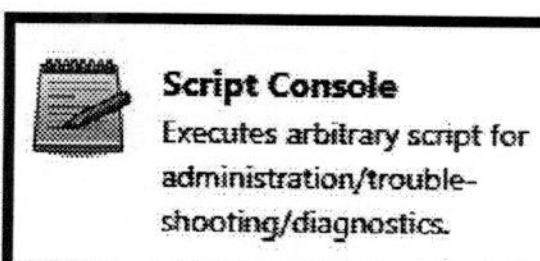

Script Console
Executes arbitrary script for administration/trouble-shooting/diagnostics.

Figure 14.17: Navigating to the Script Console

Paste the following lines in the console and click on **Run**.

```
System.clearProperty("hudson.model.DirectoryBrowserSupport.CSP");
System.setProperty("hudson.model.DirectoryBrowserSupport.CSP", "sandbox
allow-scripts; default-src 'self'; script-src * 'unsafe-eval'; img-src
*; style-src * 'unsafe-inline'; font-src *");
```

Open the Extent Report and you will now see that the report is formatted correctly.

We thus come to the end of this chapter on integration with Jenkins.

Conclusion

This chapter covered parallel execution on the Selenium Grid using Jenkins. We started off with an introduction to Jenkins. We downloaded the `jenkins.war` to the local system. We started Jenkins. We installed the Maven integration plugin and the HTML publisher plugin. We created our first job in Jenkins to execute the Cucumber framework. Finally, we executed the build from Jenkins and viewed the Extent Report in Jenkins.

This completes our journey with Cucumber. We started with an introduction to the Cucumber framework. We then integrated the framework with TestNG, Maven, and Jenkins.

To master Cucumber, you need to get used to the Gherkin Syntax, Cucumber logic flow, and try to read blogs as well as video blogs on Cucumber. Mastering Cucumber is a matter of practice and I wish you all the best in your future endeavors.

Questions

1. Explain what Jenkins is.
2. Explain the Maven integration plugin.
3. Explain the HTML publisher plugin.
4. Create a small Jenkins job to run a Maven build.
5. Configure Extent Reports in Jenkins and generate one report.

Index

E

F

G

H

I

J